LAW AND CRIME
IN THE ROMAN WORLD

What was crime in ancient Rome? Was it defined by law or social attitudes? How did damage to the individual differ from offences against the community as a whole? This book explores competing legal and extra-legal discourses in a number of areas, including theft, official malpractice, treason, sexual misconduct, crimes of violence, homicide, magic and perceptions of deviance. It argues that court practice was responsive to social change, despite the ingrained conservatism of the legal tradition, and that judges and litigants were in part responsible for the harsher operation of justice in Late Antiquity. Consideration is also given to how attitudes to crime were shaped not only by legal experts but also by the rhetorical education and practices of advocates, and by popular and even elite indifference to the finer points of law.

JILL HARRIES is Professor of Ancient History in the School of Classics at the University of St Andrews.

KEY THEMES IN ANCIENT HISTORY

EDITORS

P. A. Cartledge
Clare College, Cambridge

P. D. A. Garnsey
Jesus College, Cambridge

Key Themes in Ancient History aims to provide readable, informed and original studies of various basic topics, designed in the first instance for students and teachers of Classics and Ancient History, but also for those engaged in related disciplines. Each volume is devoted to a general theme in Greek, Roman, or where appropriate, Graeco-Roman history, or to some salient aspect or aspects of it. Besides indicating the state of current research in the relevant area, authors seek to show how the theme is significant for our own as well as ancient culture and society. By providing books for courses that are oriented around themes it is hoped to encourage and stimulate promising new developments in teaching and research in ancient history.

Other books in the series

Death-ritual and social structure in classical antiquity, by Ian Morris
0 521 37465 0 (hardback), 0 521 37611 4 (paperback)
Literacy and orality in ancient Greece, by Rosalind Thomas
0 521 37346 8 (hardback), 0 521 37742 0 (paperback)
Slavery and society at Rome, by Keith Bradley
0 521 37287 9 (hardback), 0 521 36887 7 (paperback)
Law, violence, and community in classical Athens, by David Cohen
0 521 38167 3 (hardback), 0 521 38837 6 (paperback)
Public order in ancient Rome, by Wilfried Nippel
0 521 38327 7 (hardback), 0 521 38748 3 (paperback)
Friendship in the classical world, by David Konstan
0 521 45402 6 (hardback), 0 521 45998 2 (paperback)
Sport and society in ancient Greece, by Mark Golden
0 521 496985 9 (hardback), 0 521 49790 6 (paperback)
Food and society in classical antiquity, by Peter Garnsey
0 521 64782 9 (hardback), 0 521 64588 3 (paperback)

LAW AND CRIME
IN THE ROMAN WORLD

JILL HARRIES

CAMBRIDGE
UNIVERSITY PRESS

CAMBRIDGE UNIVERSITY PRESS

Cambridge, New York, Melbourne, Madrid, Cape Town, Singapore, São Paulo

Cambridge University Press
The Edinburgh Building, Cambridge CB2 8RU, UK

Published in the United States of America by Cambridge University Press, New York

www.cambridge.org
Information in this title: www.cambridge.org/9780521535328

First published 2007

Printed in the United Kingdom at the University Press, Cambridge

A catalogue record for this publication is available from the British Library

Library of Congress Cataloguing in publication data
Harries, Jill.
Law and Crime in the Roman World / Jill Harries.
p.   cm. (Key themes in ancient history)
Includes bibliographical references and index.
ISBN 978-0-521-82820-8 (hardback) –
ISBN 978-0-521-53532-8 (paperback)
1. Roman law.   1. Title.   11. Series.
KJA147.H37   2007
340.5′4–dc22   2007016470

ISBN 978-0-521-82820-8 hardback
ISBN 978-0-521-53532-8 paperback

Contents

vii

Preface

Crime is a large topic. So too is law. The relationship of crime to law and of both to the society affected by harm done to it raises numerous issues for the lawyer, the historian and the sociologist. Crime is a moral and social, as well as a legal, problem. It therefore attracts the attention not only of legislators, the police, the courts and judges but also of modern film makers and novelists, drawn to an ever-present implied conflict between good and evil. The popularity of modern fiction on detectives in the ancient Roman world, Stephen Saylor's Gordianus the Finder and Lindsey Davis's M. Didius Falco to name but two, testifies to the abiding fascination of the figure of the detective, given extra appeal by his location in the exotic and safely distant antique world.

This book is about how the Romans thought about and discussed offences against the community, who formulated the rules and conventions about crime and how they worked. It is not therefore a manual of criminal law, and discussion is not confined to legal writers, although the ancient jurists, or legal interpreters, are extensively represented. Choice of themes has been, inevitably, selective. One is the impact of legal traditionalism on how crime was discussed and dealt with; a tension existed between legal convention and social values, which affected the ability of the discourse – though not of the judicial system – to adapt to changing perceptions of what crime was. A second is the role of litigants and court decisions under the Empire; this book suggests that sometimes they, rather than the emperors at the centre, were the motivators of changes, not always, from a modern perspective, for the better. And, thirdly, extra attention is given to perspectives on law and crime other than those of the legal specialists. Three writers are especially prominent: Quintilian, the former advocate and teacher of rhetoric under Domitian in the late first century AD; Aulus Gellius, the engaging antiquarian, from Antonine Rome; and Apuleius of Madauros in Africa, rhetor, novelist and alleged practitioner of the black arts.

I am indebted to Peter Garnsey for suggesting the topic for this book and for his support both through and since the approval process. Progress in the early stages was much assisted by my hospitable colleagues in the Department of Classics at Emory University, Atlanta, Georgia, in particular Niall Slater, whose insistence on the importance of Apuleius for the topic was crucial in the shaping of the last part of this book. I am grateful to St Andrews University and the Institute of Comparative and International Studies at Emory for their award of the Bird Exchange Fellowship, which funded my semester at Emory; in particular I would like to thank the friends at Emory who made my stay there such a delight, Gordon and Wendy Newby of ICIS, and Mary Jo Duncanson, who gave so generously of her time in showing me the sights in Atlanta and the state of Georgia. For assistance in understanding Roman law and the thinking behind it, warm thanks are due to Alan Watson, whom I visited at Athens, Georgia, and to Olivia Robinson of Glasgow, the doyenne of Roman criminal law, whose perceptive and trenchant comments over the years have been invaluable. As ever, I have profited from the kindness and collegiality of all my colleagues in Classics in St Andrews; without them this book would not have been possible.

CHAPTER I

Competing discourses

Defining crime is harder than might be expected. We all think we know what is bad or wicked or what might be termed in general usage 'criminal'. We may also have some ideas about the functions of the 'criminal justice system', and its purpose, to punish, deter and/or reform the 'criminal' and keep the law-abiding majority safe. Dissatisfaction may be expressed – to the alarm of politicians – if the system apparently fails in its purpose. Crime statistics will be offered to show progress (or not) in dealing with 'the problem of crime'; other indicators will be used to ascertain if the 'public' feel more or less safe in their homes or on the streets. 'Policing methods' may be debated and the sentences handed down by judges criticised. Moral discourse is inextricably linked with legal process: 'evil' people are expected to receive due punishment through the courts.

Crime is the concern of every citizen, and in the Roman world, as now, it may be defined, provisionally, as an offence against the community. In England the criminal is proceeded against by the state, as 'Regina (or, in Scotland, 'Her Majesty's Advocate') versus X'. At Rome, however, the role of policing was limited (Nippel 1984). Although there were 'public courts' of various kinds, there was no police authority to conduct investigations or construct 'public' prosecutions, which were largely left to the initiative of individuals. The Twelve Tables, dated to *c.* 450 BC, stated that the main responsibility for producing a defendant in court lay with the plaintiff in any action, and he was entitled to 'lay hands' on the defendant to ensure compliance (XII Tables 1.2; 3.2). This is an expression of self-help justice, which would prove remarkably durable throughout Roman history, although, as we shall see, legal procedures for the trial of 'public' offences varied considerably over time, involving People's courts, public courts, and judges sitting alone.

Variations in process evolved in parallel with the changing nature of the Roman 'community of citizens' or *civitas*. Rome grew from a small town on the Tiber, established in the eighth century BC, to a world empire, the western part of which, including Italy, ceased to exist as a political unity in the fifth century AD. The *civitas* expanded both numerically and geographically and institutions and conventions appropriate for a small face-to-face society failed to meet the needs of populations with different languages, societies and cultures, scattered over the known world from Hadrian's Wall to the Euphrates. What 'crime' was and how it was dealt with was inevitably affected by the changing role of the community and the individual within it. The evolution of law and crime is therefore also part of the story of the social and legal changes resulting from the rise (and fall) of Empire.

The story is complicated by the many forms that Roman law could take. In 44 BC Cicero defined the *ius civile*, from an advocate's point of view, as consisting of statutes passed by the people, resolutions of the Senate, decided cases, interpretations of the jurists, the edicts of magistrates, custom and equity (*Top.* 28). To these should be added, under the Empire, the legal replies and official pronouncements of emperors, which took the form of edicts, letters, rescripts and subscripts (Millar 1977; Turpin 1991). Cicero's snapshot of the forms of law in the first century BC contains a tacit acknowledgement that not all law was written down, reflecting the fact that custom and legal convention as well as self-help by individuals and family courts were essential to the self-policing of the early Roman state. Before the late second and first centuries BC there were no standing courts to try homicide, violence, forgery or corruption, but it does not follow that these offences went unpunished. As Cicero says of the rape of Lucretia, it was obviously unlawful in terms of 'natural law', although there was no written law against it (*Leg.* 2.10; cf. *Rep.* 2.46). The resultant expulsion of the Tarquins in 510 BC was perhaps the most extreme case of the community's punishing offences against itself by direct action.

LEGAL DISCOURSES

To define 'crime' as an offence against the community is to beg many questions. Who decides what is damaging to the community, as opposed to what harms an individual? What is the difference between 'crime' and 'wrongdoing' and will the lawyer's answer be consistent with social perceptions? How could new 'crimes' be assimilated into the legal system? What was the relationship overall between legal discourse and morality? Who were in control of the discourse in the first place?

Crime can be studied as a purely legal construct; it was what the lawyers said it was. An essential point to understand about Roman law is that its primary purpose was to provide remedies by defining the legal processes by which a legal remedy could be sought to compensate for some alleged wrong or injury, or achieve resolution of a dispute. Thus an offence defined by law as subject to 'public' legal process was a 'crime'. It follows, as a general point about legal discourse, that the existence of law is a precondition for the existence of crime. No 'law' means no 'crime', because crime could exist only in the context of the legal process set up to deal with it. It would also follow from this that discussion of law and crime would be confined to a group of texts, with their own assumptions and agenda. Change over time would be acknowledged, but only in the terms of discourse imposed by the texts themselves.

If, in line with a provisional definition of crime as an offence to be prosecuted in the public courts, we list Roman crimes in terms of public procedure, we emerge with a restricted and somewhat arbitrary list, consisting, for example, of treason, murder – specifically knifing and poisoning – forgery, adultery, peculation, kidnapping and electoral corruption. These acquired standing courts (*quaestiones*) from 149 BC onwards and the list became fixed, to apply even after the courts had ceased to function, at some point before the third century AD. The canon remained operational in Justinian's collection of extracts from juristic writings, assembled as the Digest (D.) in AD 533; 'public' offences were covered in Book 48 (out of fifty). This excludes many forms of wrongdoing which we might assume to be 'criminal', such as theft, fraud, injurious behaviour, robbery with violence and some kinds of murder (e.g. of a slave), as well as what we might term 'white-collar crime', such as embezzlement. But such assumptions are both anachronistic and based not on legal assumptions but social values.

Privileging purely 'legal' discourse raises other problems for the historian. Our subject would be redefined as 'the law of crime', and analysis would be confined to a select group of texts, created and subsequently excerpted and codified by specialists. Although the legal interpreters, or jurists, on whose writings so much of modern understanding of law is based, were not especially interested in public criminal law (because, in theory, the public owned it), they worked within a legal framework which could be self-referential to a fault. Law had its own traditions, not invariably shared by the movers of changes in criminal, especially penal, policy. The excerpted imperial juristic texts in the Digest of Justinian are fragmentary and arranged to create a single, coherent narrative of law. It is deceptively easy to view the interpretative tradition as continuous and uniform, because that was the impression Justinian sought to create. In fact, from the Late Republic to the Late Empire, the legal interpreters responded (or failed to respond) to several changes in judicial practice, while also seeking to assert unbroken continuity with the past. The end result was a narrative, given final shape by Justinian, which is traditionalist, Rome-centred, despite the impact of Empire, and dependent on the structures of a political and judicial past which, by the second century AD, no longer existed.

There were also tensions between different types of law. Early imperial legal thought inherited a system of civil law, based on the Praetor's Edict and the *ius civile*, or law of citizens, which regulated Romans in their dealings with each other (and also, through various ingenious devices, with non-Romans). A conflict would come to exist within the legal establishment (which included the emperor) between the culture of civil procedures, which regulated recompense or compensation, including awards that were 'penal', and the 'revenge' culture of parts of the public 'criminal' law. One story to be told of the evolution of Roman law is the incorporation into public criminal procedures of unlawful acts largely dealt with under civil procedures while Rome was a Republic.

CRIME AND SOCIETY

Is crime purely a social construct? Killing, for example, may be acceptable if it is an enemy who is killed, or unlawful if it is a neighbour or fellow-citizen (although accident or provocation might still be taken into account). Adultery was (and is) punishable by death under some legal systems but is no longer so in modern Britain. Moreover, formal legal sanctions are not the only means by which society may punish offenders. Social pressure may isolate the offender against its values, making continued existence within the group impossible, but without resort to legal process.

In the case of the Romans, the social approach is attractive because it privileges the moral terminology which the Romans attached to actions they found socially unacceptable or threatening and therefore deserving of punishment in some sense, by public or private process, extra-legal jurisdiction (such as that of the *pater familias* over the family) or social ostracism. The moral discourse of the Romans had numerous words for bad behaviour and wrongdoing: *scelus* (villainy), *facinus* (bad action), *nefas* (evil action), *peccatum* (bad action, later the Christian word for sin), *maleficium* (something done badly) and *delictum* (moral failure), to name but a few (for more, see Riess 2001: 32–44). Some of these, notably *maleficium* and *delictum*, were imported into legal discourse as well and acquired technical meanings. Even used technically, loose vocabulary encouraged misunderstanding. Gaius, for example, described as *maleficium* wrongful intent on the part of a substitute heir, in the relatively innocuous context of disputes arising if the original heir died in the lifetime of the testator (*Inst.* 2.81). But he also termed a criminal conviction under the Lex Cornelia as *maleficium*, observing that it was one of the grounds on which citizenship could become forfeit (*Inst.* 1.128). As Gaius' contemporaries also labelled magic as a *maleficium*, there was clearly scope for confusion between the 'criminal' and merely 'civil'.

The legal discourse on badness was primarily concerned not with moral castigation but with legal remedies. It therefore focused on the word from which the English 'crime' would be derived. This was *crimen*, which meant not 'crime' but 'reproach' and, in both legal and moral discourse, 'accusation'. The law on 'crime' was defined in terms not of a hierarchy of offences but of the nature of the accusations that could be brought and the procedural and penal consequences of so doing for both accuser and accused. The Romans therefore did have a vocabulary for what might be termed 'crime' in a moral sense but there was no one word for 'crime' in Roman law. Instead, the procedure, through public accusation, served as a form of signal as to the nature of the offence. The 'accuser' asked the public, through its courts, to hold the accused to account.

But events once a public case reached the courts were far from predictable. Under the public *quaestio* system operated in the Late Republic at Rome, the panels of judges (*iudices*), although drawn from the elite, were not necessarily experts in any aspect of public criminal law, nor could they expect to receive legal guidance from the presiding magistrate, whose job was to ensure that procedures were correctly observed. The rhetorical strategies of Cicero, and later Quintilian, who practised as an advocate before turning to education, allowed generous space for interpretation of statute as well as concentration on the characters of the accused and accusers. Cicero later acknowledged that his defence of Cluentius, charged in 66 BC by a group including his mother, Sassia, with various crimes, had fooled the jury (Quint. *Inst.* 2.17.21); his technique was to vilify the 'unnatural' Sassia and her now dead husband, Oppianicus, at considerable length, destroying the moral credibility of the prosecution as a whole. The *quaestio* process encouraged the development of forensic oratory. When the *quaestio* was superseded by hearings before a single judge (*cognitio*), advocates and speechmakers still had a role. However, under *cognitio* the tendency was for advocates and legal representatives to resort to techniques of cross-examination rather than emotive appeals.

Where Roman law showed the clearest traces of the social values of the elite law-givers was in its treatment of honour and shame. Several forms of civil dispute hinged on trust or good faith (*bona fides*), and improper behaviour was castigated also in moral terms; investment of gains made dishonestly in a partnership, for example, were stigmatised as a 'shameful and disgusting co-operation in wrongdoing' (Ulpian, at D. 17.1.53, *delictorum turpis ac foeda communio*). Losing the legal argument even in civil disputes under the Republic could damage reputation (*existimatio*) but under the Empire *infamia* became a formal legal sanction, including not only disgrace but also the loss of civil rights (D. 3.22.1). It applied to the soldier dishonourably discharged; the man who failed to discharge his legal obligations; the thief and the robber by violence; even, in Late Antiquity, the bigamist (*Codex Justinianus* (*CJ*) 5.5.2.11; 9.9.18). And some actions were disgraceful, even if legal; Ulpian advised that a man who had hidden away a prostitute for lust was not liable for kidnapping or theft but nonetheless acted more 'shamefully' than either kidnapper or thief and so would incur social 'ignominy', which more than made up for the lack of legal redress (D. 47.2.39).

It was not necessary to have done something wrong at all to incur *infamia*, because being 'infamous' was a state of being. It was a status attached, for example, to professions, the exercise of which would automatically entail 'shameful' behaviour. For example, owners of brothels, taverns and bathhouses, which openly or covertly engaged in the sex trade, were categorised as guilty of pimping (*lenocinium*) and were therefore *infames* (D. 3.2.4.2–3). The 'infamous' were not, therefore, the same as the lower of the two social classes, the *humiliores*, identified from the second century AD onwards as being less legally privileged than their superiors, the *honestiores*. However, the two 'less honourable' social and legal statuses could operate together to disadvantage the would-be litigant of lower status. The rule on the legal action for cheating (*dolus*) by 'devious and dishonest' types (Ulpian at D. 4.3.1), which entailed *infamia* for the guilty, was that it was to be used only where other actions for dishonesty were not available. An additional restriction was that an action could not be brought by a social inferior against a superior, nor could a 'dissolute, spendthrift or otherwise unworthy' character prosecute someone of superior respectability (D. 4.3.11.1), although other, lesser actions not entailing *infamia* could be used. Thus the elite lawmakers looked after their own, denying to lesser (and by association less virtuous) people choice of legal remedy.

The moral also impinged on the philosophical and other manifestations of the elite culture from which all legislators and commentators were drawn. Jurists were, on the whole, practical people, concerned with solutions to specific problems arrived at by the manipulation of rules, but philosophical discourse also had its place in the promotion of the discipline. When the Severan jurist Ulpian claimed that law was a true philosophy (D. 1.1.1.1), or his older contemporary Papinian translated Demosthenes on law as the expression of the public will (D. 1.3.1; cf. the original at 1.3.2) or jurists in general cited Homer or Xenophon or other classical writers (e.g. Gaius, *On the Twelve Tables*, at D. 50.16.233; Just. *Inst.* 4.18.5), they asserted their shared identity with their cultivated readership. And they shared a common enemy, the doer of bad actions, deserving of punishment or at least social censure.

JURISTS AND THE PAST

The existence of two separate discourses, the social and the legal, inevitably created tension between legal provision and social expectations of appropriate punishments for the 'wicked'. How was a 'public' offence to be defined? How could the law respond to changing social perceptions of (for example) religious or sexual 'deviance'? If the law failed to change in line with social values, or the agenda of those charged with administering the criminal law, a point could be reached at which legal procedures, established in a different geographical and temporal context, could fail to satisfy the requirements of rulers for order, and of citizens for protection against perceived threats.

The evolution of public justice under the Empire was shaped by a creative tension between observance of the legal tradition and innovations which were enabled through the flexibility of court practice and the power of emperors and (to a lesser extent) provincial governors to act as they wished. As radical reform was institutionally impossible and an unacceptable breach of continuity with the past, flexibility was in practice created through the *cognitio* procedure, which was conducted, not by a group of jurors representing the public, but by a single judge, who had wide discretion. The *cognitio* process was probably always the norm in the provinces, where the provincial governor or his deputy presided, along with his *consilium*, and quickly became so at Rome, as the *quaestiones* gradually closed down and their business was transferred to the Prefect of the City. Despite this, jurists in the second century embarked on the production of a series of treatises on the *publica iudicia*, the public courts, even though those courts, apart from perhaps the adultery court, were no longer in existence.

Jurists were prisoners of their past and the legal tradition in which they worked. The location at Rome of second-century AD jurists, such as Gaius (probably) and Pomponius, and a prevailing antiquarian culture affected perspectives; Gaius composed a commentary on the Twelve Tables and Pomponius a treatise on the *De iure civili* of Q. Mucius Scaevola, written in the 80s BC. Treatises on the *publica iudicia* (Bauman 1996: 115–23) do not appear to have been composed before the reign of Antoninus Pius, apart from one book in a work with significant antiquarian content by Ateius Capito in the reign of Augustus (Gell. *NA* 4.14; 10.6). Under Pius there appeared two juristic studies of the 'public judgements', one by L. Volusius Maecianus, later Prefect of Egypt, in fourteen books, and a shorter effort by Venuleius Saturninus in three, which discussed among other things judicial discretion in the punishment of slaves (D. 48.2.12). According to Ulpian (D. 48.9.6), Maecianus, of whom only three fragments survive in direct quotation, recorded that the punishment for parricide under the Lex Pompeia should be inflicted on the accomplices of the murderer. He also quoted with approval the judgement of the legate Trebius Germanus that an under-age slave, who had failed to raise the alarm when his master was attacked even though he slept at the foot of his bed, should be executed, even though he was under age, as he could have saved his master (D. 29.5.14) – an example of a non-imperial court decision affecting legal practice. For Maecianus, Rome was still the focus of judicial discourse, despite its diminishing relevance to judicial practice in the provinces: the Lex Julia on public violence, he wrote (D. 48.6.8), protected defendants from being forcibly prohibited from reporting for trial at a stated time at Rome.

The choice to write a book about a set of courts now probably obsolete, especially when taken by a prominent imperial careerist such as Maecianus, is significant. Both he and Venuleius Saturninus would have hoped to shape a new discourse on public offences as a distinct category in the judicial system. In so doing, they imposed a spurious uniformity on the offences covered by the Republican *quaestiones*, which did not match the facts. As we shall see (chapters 4 and 5), features of the original People's courts, such as that anyone could accuse, were not invariably adopted, and the penalties were not all the same either. But by creating a literature on the *publica iudicia*, Maecianus, Saturninus and their successors under the Severans set up a sort of canon of offences, which were categorised as 'public' and treated as such in legal hearings. The *publica iudicia* continued to require the presence of an accuser, whom the defendant had a right to confront, and the lodging of a formal document of 'inscription', written in due form and signed by the accuser or another, if he was illiterate (D. 48.2.3.2); by Late Antiquity the accuser 'bound himself' by inscription also to suffer the same penalty as the accused if his charge failed.

In a procedural sense, therefore, the separation of the *publica iudicia* from the rest had real practical significance. However, because the criteria were based on the distant past, the separation also risked alienating the legal process from changes in social perceptions of what damaged the community and therefore deserved public punishment. Moreover, Maecianus and Saturninus wrote within a few years of Salvius Julianus' revision and codification of the Praetor's Edict, as instructed by Hadrian, perhaps in 130 AD. They may well have been influenced by his project, as his codification was followed up with an extensive work of interpretation, consisting of a Digest of ninety books. Two kinds of *ordo* were thus created, the *ordo* of matters covered by the Edict, and the *ordo* of the *publica iudicia* and their statutes.

The idea of an *ordo*, therefore, is, in this context, a product of juristic discourse. The purpose of the concept was to provide a sense of system and order. While Maecianus and his colleagues at the time and later were not writing as official codifiers of public law, the effect was to create a fixed body of knowledge. But as any codifier or systematiser of law would find, the next thing to happen would be attempts to modify existing contents of the 'code' or add new ones. It was these new problems requiring remedies which required jurisdiction 'outside the order', *extra ordinem*. The conservatism of legal discourse was thus accommodated, but at a price, and that price has been paid also by modern scholarship, which uses as a collective term for this process of adaptation, the *cognitio extra ordinem*. This term will be avoided as far as possible in what follows (but see below, chapter 3, pp. 29–33), not because of its dubious Latinity – Latin does not like to attach prepositional phrases to nouns – but because the term is itself a product of a specialised discourse and its meaning is thus open to misinterpretation.

THE COUNTER-CULTURES

One further disjunction between legal discourse and social attitudes must also be acknowledged. Although the elite law-makers at Rome and administrators of public criminal justice dominate the record, they were open to challenge. Crowds did not always react as expected (see Foucault 1977: 59–69 on executions). Legal commentators acknowledged that certain types of hooligan could even be popular; if the 'Boys', wrote the Severan Callistratus, have done nothing worse than stir things a little, 'pandering to the applause of the mob', they should simply be given a mild beating and/ or banned from attending public entertainments in future (D. 48.19.28.3).

The nocturnal activities of less appealing hoodlums were recorded by Suetonius, with reference to Nero (Suet. *Nero* 26), and Apuleius (*Met.* 2.18).

Champions of counter-cultures asserted an alternative world-view in other ways: the literature which promoted illicit love as a form of celebration of adultery, made a public offence by Augustus in 18 BC, the cheeky exploits of the bandit Bulla Felix in Italy in the early 200s AD, as recorded by Dio (*Epitome*, 77.10), and the Christian denials of the powers of the pagan gods, maintained through public martyrdom down to 313 AD, were all challenges to the official consensus as expressed by the elite exponents of Roman law. Nor did they exist in isolation. Ovid's 'didactic' work on adultery, the *Ars Amatoria*, intended as a joke but interpreted as a challenge to Augustus, mattered because it had readers; Bulla Felix struck a chord because he satirised the Roman judicial system, impersonating Roman officials and asserting that the prefect was no more than a bandit himself; Christian martyr-acts asserted, to the bemusement of those who heard them, that people executed as criminals in the arena had a privileged passage to the afterlife.

The figure of the bandit (Shaw 1984) represented what organised society was not and as such was fascinating to writers on exotic subjects remote from real life. It was argued by Hobsbawn (1969) that the 'social bandit' flourished with the support of his community (or part of it), preying on the rich to redistribute wealth to the poor, as Bulla Felix allegedly did. Certainly some bandits were an integral part of how their neighbourhood functioned: in Late Antiquity Isaurian mafias ran effective protection rackets for the mutual benefit of themselves and the local landowners (Hopwood 1989), and in fifth-century Gaul the citizens of Auxerre preferred coexistence with their local Bacaudae to assistance from an imperially sponsored Alan warlord (Constantius, *Life of Germanus* 6.28). But in much literary discourse the figure of the bandit is subsumed by other agendas. For the novelist (Hopwood 1998), the bandit inhabited inaccessible places, such as the marshes of the Nile Delta or remote mountain caves. In Apuleius a band of robbers establish an alternative state, with a treasury (*fiscus, Met.* 7.10.1) and decrees (*Met.* 6.26.5).

For those public figures who claimed to speak for the virtuous majority, the otherness of the bandit could be ascribed to such individuals as Catiline, Clodius and Antonius, the political rivals of Cicero from the 60s to the 40s BC, or the opponents in Galilee of the controversial Josephus in the 60s AD (Isaac 1984; Shaw 1993). So pervasive is the 'establishment' representation of all social and political movements to which the writer or speaker is opposed that it is often not possible to establish the motives or composition of supposedly 'bandit' enterprises, (on local self-help movements in Gaul, see Van Dam 1985). For what all 'bandits' had in common was that they were outside the protection of the law and their repression was a policing matter. In Late Antiquity part of what schoolchildren could expect to see in the Forum was the summary trial, torture and execution of a bandit whose very presence before the tribunal was proof of his guilt (Dionisotti 1982).

CONCLUSION

The legal tradition was faced with the problem of adapting to shifting values and expectations, while retaining its distinctive traditions; under the Empire the retention of formerly vital distinctions between the 'civil' and the 'public' was imperilled by misunderstanding, indifference to the finer points of law, the requirements of litigants, and the responses of judges and the imperial administration. A system designed by Romans for Rome was forced to adapt to the requirements of the 'world city'. The law on crime, in its broad sense, had many 'stakeholders': the Republican authors of the public criminal statutes; the jurists who interpreted offences under the civil and later the criminal law; the judges, singular and plural, who composed or presided over the criminal courts; the advocates, whose priority was persuasion, not exposition; the litigants in search of compensation or revenge; and, from the first century AD, the imperial legislator conscious of his image as the hard-line 'avenger' of evil. And beyond them all was a shadowy sense that the criminal law, being originally aimed at offences against the public good, should also benefit from public support, that it should be, as Papinian (following Demosthenes) said of statute (*lex*), 'an enactment of the community ... a communal agreement of the whole state' (D. 1.3.1).

CHAPTER 2

Public process and the legal tradition

At the end of the first century BC the collective rule of the Senate and People of Rome gave way to the sole rule of Augustus and his successors, whose autocracy became increasingly overt. The constitutional practices of the Roman Republic had distributed the power to frame, pass and interpret legislation over a number of different authorities: the priesthoods, charged with interpreting sacred and public law; the magistrates, who could enforce obedience and initiate legislation before the People (Lintott 1999a: 94–102); the Senate, whose collective authority gave more weight to their decrees (*consulta*) than their formal advisory status might imply (1999a: 65–88); and the popular assemblies themselves, whose enactments were binding on the whole *res publica* from the third century BC onwards (1999a: 40–64). The application of public criminal law in practice was also affected by the pleading of advocates in court, interpreting both written text and legal convention in the interests of their clients.

The advent of imperial rule brought no immediate formal change; Augustus operated within the letter of the Republican constitutional framework. The reality, however, was that the powers of the main magistracies were vested in one man, the emperor, who could also control other magistrates, Senate deliberations and, through them, what remained of popular legislative authority. Power over law therefore passed to the emperor and his advisers. But emperors could not do everything. A powerful tradition of learned interpretation of the *ius civile* existed independently of imperial authority, guarded and expanded by the jurists; a separate, but related body of civil law (*ius honorarium*) was developed through the Praetorian Edict and its related commentaries. The seriousness with which emperors took their control of law in the second century is shown by Hadrian's 'codification' of the Praetor's Edict, ordaining that any future modifications should be made by the emperor (reported at Justinian, *Constitutio Tanta* 18); at the same time, if not earlier, the jurists were brought into the imperial *consilium* and thus became an extension of the imperial will. By the fourth century the independent legal expert had become invisible, concealed behind the formidable rhetoric of imperial legal pronouncements (constitutions), and the tradition of civil-law exposition he represented was subsumed by an all-pervasive imperial bureaucracy.

Roman law existed in many forms, and a number of interest groups were involved in its formulation. It is therefore difficult to envisage it as the coherent entity that use of 'law' in the singular implies. Throughout Roman history there was competition to control its content and its administration or enforcement. Under the Republic, senators competed with each other, the priests (who were also senators) competed with the magistrates (who were sometimes also priests), and the jurists with the advocates. After Augustus the emperor should have been above competition. But law – as Theodosius II acknowledged in the 420s AD (*CJ* 1.14.4) – was above emperors, and emperors could not be seen to disrespect the legal tradition or its self-appointed guardians, the learned senators, the jurists, the experts in the tradition of the praetorian law and the *ius civile*.

Two other sources of influence are more difficult to analyse but, for the criminal law in action, no less significant. What actually happened in court is one. Court decisions, unless made by emperors, did not create formal precedents, although evidence from Egypt shows that previous court decisions of Prefects could be cited to guide verdicts in later hearings (Katzoff 1972, 1980). But the responsive nature of imperial legal rulings, through the rescripts sent as replies to legal queries, allowed judges to push for their own agendas, such as innovations to the penal system (below, chapter 3) or the creation of new offences specific to a particular locality (cf. D. 47.11.9, Arabia; 10, Egypt). And judges, whether sitting alone or as members of a panel, could be influenced by factors which had nothing to do with law, factors such as the social standing of the parties, or the antics of a hysterical mob, baying for the blood of the Christians, or others seen as social deviants.

The second and yet more difficult aspect is the power of the customary, which was often also unwritten. Roman legal thought always gave space in its concept of 'law' to what was customary (but not necessarily written down). Legal custom (see D. 1.3 *passim*) could be more strictly defined with reference to a legal tradition. Ulpian referred to the *mos* of 'our citizen community' on wards and guardians (D. 29.2.8.pr), and Modestinus, a pupil of Ulpian, referred to the punishment for parricide established 'by ancestral custom' (D. 48.9.9). This could include local usages in the provinces, provided that it could be clearly established what the custom was. It was also possible to resort to wider definitions of custom based on social values. Salvius Julianus, codifier of the Praetorian Edict (with ninety-book commentary) and consul in 148, observed (D. 1.3.32) that, just as statutes were binding because they reflected the popular will, so what the *populus*, People, had approved through its actions, without writing, was also universally valid.

IUDICIUM POPULI

Roman citizens (and others) required protection from harm. Those whose wrongdoing was seen as damaging to society as a whole, which included certain forms of harm inflicted on individuals, could expect to be punished under 'public' procedure known as the 'judgement of the People', the *iudicium populi*. The early Roman community was small enough for the *populus* to act directly to protect itself through hearings at which the People were themselves the adjudicators. By the Late Republic this versatile process had become subsumed by a selective historical tradition which laid particular emphasis on 'political' crimes, such as *perduellio*, treason. The key feature of the proceedings was that the debates on the facts were open to all, but the final judgement rested with a formally constituted assembly of the People.

The process first entailed notice of 'the day' of the trial, the charge that was to be brought and perhaps the penalty requested. At this early stage the magistrates, as representatives of the community, were to the fore: the prosecutors recorded by the Livian tradition were all tribunes of the plebs, aediles, both curule and plebeian, or quaestors. Second, there were three investigative hearings, with set intervals between them, conducted by a magistrate before a *contio*, or assembly of the people, which anyone could attend. Third, after a further interval, the magistrate pronounced sentence and the accused, if found guilty, could exercise his right of appeal (*provocatio*) to the People, who could reject or amend the magistrate's decision. Where the penalty requested was a fine, the tribal assembly decided the outcome; in capital cases the People were convened in the Comitia Centuriata, the Assembly of the Centuries (Cic. *Sest.* 65; *Rep.* 2.61; *Leg.* 3.11 and 44; Jones 1972: 1–39; Lintott 1999a: 149–57).

But how were 'public' offences to be defined? Some were obvious. The first and worst of crimes in early Rome would have been *perduellio*, betrayal of the state, which later authorities construed etymologically (Gaius, *On the Twelve Tables* (second century AD) at D. 50.16.234); it was the behaviour of an 'enemy' (*perduellis*), the consequence of which was the expulsion of the traitor from the community, by execution or other means. But a significant number of the *perduellio* prosecutions recorded concern holders of office and *imperium*, who had failed to carry out their duties and so damaged the public good (see below, pp. 72–3).

As bad as treason, because it offended against the central Roman value of *pietas*, was the killing of a close relation (*parricidium*; Cloud 1971). This was no ordinary homicide but a 'transgression fondamentale' (Y. Thomas 1981: 645) of the social and religious order, on a par with treason (Briquel 1980). Two special quaestors for *parricidium* were probably responsible for prosecuting this offence. Tradition prescribed the 'penalty of the sack' (*poena cullei*) for the parricide. He was flogged, sewn up and thrown into the sea, thus being removed from contact with all the elements (Cic. *Rosc. Am.* 25.70–26.72). The sack may also have contained a bizarre assortment of other living creatures, such as a rooster, dog, serpent and monkey.

How far the presence of the sack in the discourse of punishment reflects the extent of its use in practice cannot be known. Hadrian conceded that execution by wild beasts in the arena could be substituted for the 'sack' if no sea was conveniently available (D. 48.9.9. pr.), and murderers of close kin were threatened with the 'sack' by Constantine (*Codex Theodosianus* (*CT*) 9.15.1, of 319). Quintus Cicero put two people into sacks when governor of Asia (Cic. *Q. fr.* 1.2.2.5), an action which illustrates the discretionary powers of punishment available to governors. The symbolic power of the sack as a punishment for the very wicked, which effectively excluded them from the community in death, as in life, was invoked by Juvenal against adulterers (*Sat.* 10, 317), an idea picked up by the fourth-century emperor Constans, who exploited the rhetoric of punishment to threaten adulterers with the 'sack', as if they too were parricides (*CT* 11.36.4).

The identification of what was 'criminal', that is, an offence against the public good, was nominally a reflection of the public will. As it was up to the community to decide not only on guilt but also on the nature of criminality itself, it was not necessary that a statute should be in place to outlaw wrongdoing. As offences against the family, which could not always be controlled by family courts, could be seen as damaging the public good, the *populus* heard cases involving unlawful sex (*stuprum*): Valerius Maximus, an anthologiser of moral tales, records the prosecution before the People for *stuprum* of one C. Scantinius Capitolinus by the curule aedile, M. Claudius Marcellus, in the 220s BC (Val. Max. 6.1.7; cf. Plut. *Marc.* 2) and, in the early first century, the conviction of Cn. Sergius Silus for trying to corrupt a married woman with a bribe (Val. Max. 6.1.8). The wide remit of the *iudicia populi* was illustrated by Pliny the Elder in the first century AD, when he remarked that even matters agricultural could be brought before the People's court (*Natural History* 18.41–3). A humble, but hard-working farmer, a Greek freedman called C. Furius Chresimus, was prosecuted by a curule aedile for magicking the crops of his (less efficient but far richer) neighbours onto his land with enchantments (*veneficia*), behaviour specifically outlawed by the Twelve Tables (Gordon 1999: 253–4). Frightened that his powerful adversaries might secure a conviction, Chresimus brought before the court his agricultural implements and his healthy, well-clothed and happy workers; these, he said, were his 'enchantments', along with something he could not show the court, his long hours and the sweat of his brow. He was unanimously acquitted.

The ideology of the People's court, that the *populus* could hear any case that it regarded as 'criminal', subject to the willingness of a tribune or other prosecutor to act on their behalf, was as significant – and more durable – than the form that the 'court' or its procedure might take at any given time. It gave legitimacy to future litigants, courts and judges who – subject to certain constraints – had wide discretion in practice in the defining or redefining of offences as 'public' or criminal. The principle of flexibility in the definition of what was 'criminal' outlasted the formal constitutional powers of both *contio* and *populus*.

When the standing *quaestiones* were set up at Rome, their creators did not envisage their expansion beyond the capital. The concepts behind their procedures were therefore those of the Roman Forum. There the presiding magistrate would sit on his tribunal accompanied by his *consilium*, assessors and, at appropriate points, the panel of judges (*iudices*) chosen from the album, created in line with statute at the start of his year of office. The *iudices* were required to be domiciled at Rome or within a mile of the city (*Roman Statutes* (*RS*) I, 86–7 and 99), a limit which may have been expanded later but which was obviously inapplicable outside Italy. The provision became part of the legal tradition long after it had ceased to operate in practice; Ulpian recorded a similar regulation for the selection of the adjudicators of homicide cases (*Collatio of Roman and Mosaic Law* 1.3 = Lenel (1889): 976, no. 2194).

THE *QUAESTIO*-STATUTES

In the mid second century BC an important innovation changed the nature and direction of 'public procedures' for ever. Beginning with the Lex Calpurnia on extortion (*repetundae*, lit. restitution) in 149 BC, the Roman elite embarked on an exercise in self-regulation through the establishment of a number of standing courts, set up to 'investigate' offences against the public interest. These were called *quaestiones* and were a continuation of earlier *ad hoc* 'boards of enquiry' set up by the higher magistrates to investigate scandals and outbreaks of criminality as they occurred, especially in Italy (Polybius 6.13.4–5; Livy 39.38.3; 40.37 and 43; 40.44). They therefore derived from a tradition of jurisdiction different from that of the *iudicium populi*, where hearings were conducted by magistrates without *imperium*.

However, as the *iudicium populi* fell out of use, the standing *quaestiones* also came to be known as *publica iudicia*. They did not formally replace the People's courts and in some respects were less satisfactory. They were less flexible as a means of controlling bad behaviour, as their remit was limited to the offence defined in the statute which set up the court; they did not therefore allow for such responses as that of the Senate to the 'Bacchanalian conspiracy' in 186 BC, which investigated and punished extensive malpractices carried out under cover of the cult, and regulated its conduct for the future (Livy 39.8–19; *FIRA* 1.30). As each *quaestio* was set up or modified in the light of contemporary events and possibly ephemeral political considerations, the selection of bad actions covered was arbitrary. And there were often short-term political considerations at work. The law on 'restitution' (extortion), which held senatorial provincial governors to account, was especially politicised, and changes in the composition of their panels of judges occurred frequently from the tribunate of C. Gracchus in 123/2 onwards (see below, pp. 64–5). As political, and even more dangerous, was the Lex Appuleia of the tribune Saturninus (100 BC), establishing the accusation of 'damaging the greatness of the Roman People', *maiestas laesa*, which would come to supersede *perduellio* as the statute governing treason (below, chapter 6, pp. 72–5).

In 81-80 the dictator L. Cornelius Sulla made the first serious attempt to provide a coherent organisation for the *quaestiones*, which had hitherto developed piecemeal. Three of his statutes, the Lex Cornelia on cut-throats (*sicarii*) and poisoners (*venefici*), the Lex Cornelia on forgery (*de falsis*), and a law on outrage (*iniuria*), which may not have set up a *quaestio*, were to survive the test of time. In the two generations which followed, legislators continued to create and modify public accusations by statute: new laws were passed on parricide (the Lex Pompeia), which probably redefined the offence as the killing of any near relation (Robinson 1995: 47); violence, public and private; peculation; extortion; maladministration of the *annona*, the supply of grain which fed the Roman people; corruption (*ambitus*); kidnapping (the Lex Fabia, of unknown date); and *maiestas*. All these were reworked and redefined, most notably by Caesar and later Augustus, who also, controversially, in 18 BC made adultery a crime punishable by public process (see below, chapter 7).

PROCESS AT ROME

When the legal draftsmen of the Republican *quaestio* laws, of which the Gracchan *Lex Repetundarum* is a representative sample, took the trouble to devote long, often repetitive and stylistically obscure paragraphs to legal process, then added further effort by inscribing them on bronze or other tablets for all to read who could, they did so for a reason. Process mattered because it set out the duties and obligations of all the people involved in a prosecution, explained how they were to act, how the verdict was to be arrived at, and what were to be the consequences for the accused. Public prosecutions could be initiated at Rome under the Republic from early in the year (after the album had been formed) down to 1 September (*Lex Rep.* 9), after which there was a risk that a change of praetor would disrupt proceedings (*Lex Rep.* 7). Some cases, such as the trial of Manilius for public violence, were heard after the September deadline. The order in which cases were taken was probably decided by the date when the action was brought but cases could be accelerated if they were connected with another (Cic. *Clu.* 56) or especially serious (Cic. *Inv.* 2.58).

The first step was *postulatio*, a request to the magistrate for permission to bring the charge. Although in cases described as 'public' there was a theory that 'whoever wishes' could prosecute, in practice those eligible might be defined and restricted by statute (*Lex Rep.* 1–2) or there might exist another with a better claim to initiate an action (as could be the case under Augustus' adultery law). If more than one prosecutor presented himself, the magistrate and a panel of adjudicators held a preliminary hearing, or divination, to decide who should bring the prosecution; Cicero's *Divinatio in Caecilium* is a rare example of the type of pleading employed in what was an exceptionally high-profile case, the prosecution of Verres in 70 BC. The losers could still participate in a supporting role as sub-prosecutors or *subscriptores*.

Once the identity of the prosecutor had been agreed, the name of the accused and the charge against him could be lodged with the magistrate; this was *nominis delatio*. At this stage, the prosecution could be held up if the accused was a holder of public office at the time (*Lex Rep.* 8–9), or absent on state business. Assuming that he was present, the magistrate would satisfy himself that there was a case to answer and then proceed to supervise the formal lodging of the *inscriptio*. This defined the charge and therefore the *quaestio* before which it would be brought. Multiple charges were not allowed. This eased the situation of the defendant somewhat, as he knew what to expect. Those brought to trial before the Senate suffered from the fear that an unexpected charge might be added to the main indictment to confuse the issue and make conviction more likely.

After the case had been accepted by the magistrate (*nominis receptio*), a date was set for the full hearing before the *iudices* in the Forum. There was a minimum notice period of nine days (Asc. *Corn.* 59C, Greenidge 1901/ 1971: 466–8) but a longer interval could be allowed, especially in *repetundae* cases, where it would be necessary to travel to the province to collect evidence (while the accused governor used the interval to enlist his friends both at Rome and in the province itself). Cicero had 110 days for the Verres case, of which he used 60. Once the full hearing was convened in the Forum, it proceeded to judgement with a formal vote, even when the accused had failed to appear. Milo, for example, was condemned in absence, as were the assassins of Caesar by Octavian's tribunal in 43 BC.

In the Roman Forum our trial would compete with several other trials being held simultaneously. Republican justice was both public and rowdy and there was little sense that the jurors might require a period of quiet reflection. Indeed, both setting and structure may have served to confuse them further. Judges in public trials were required to hear the arguments before they were confronted with the evidence. Speeches setting out the facts of the case and their lines of argument were made, first by the prosecution *patronus* (advocate) and then by the defence, both of whom were subject to time limits. Both sides then engaged in cross-questioning or interrogating the other (a skill at which the quick-witted Cicero excelled) before moving to the calling of witnesses. At no point did the judge offer a legal summing up or directions to the jury about what the law was or what questions should properly be addressed. Nowadays, in British courts, the judge's summing up is crucial (as I know from personal experience as a *iudex*) and the jurors are entitled to a period of quiet reflection and discussion, and to take as long as they wish to reach a verdict. These luxuries were not available to the Roman juror.

Finally, the adjudicators were asked for their decision. The ballots offered two choices, 'A' for acquittal and 'C' for condemnation, and jurors were expected to cast their votes independently; there was no scope for retirement to a private room or consideration of a collective verdict. But jurors could also announce that the case was not proven and that they were unable to reach a decision ('*non liquet*'). The *Lex Repetundarum* threatened the indecisive with fines (*Lex Rep.* 46–8) and allowed a vote to take place once two-thirds had made up their minds; if there was a tie, the accused was acquitted. But a device adopted later to avoid stalemate was the use of adjournment (*comperendinatio*), allowing a second hearing (*actio*), at which the advocates could revisit the evidence and even call new witnesses, if appropriate. Cicero's speeches in defence of three allegedly corrupt gover-nors, Fonteius, Flaccus and Scaurus, all appear to relate to the second *actio* and revisit evidence and arguments already advanced, with a view to confirmation or rebuttal.

Augustus' law on the *publica iudicia* overhauled and simplified Republican procedure (Bauman 1980; Santalucia 1998: 189–93). The *postu-latio* and *divinatio* stages were subsumed into the simple lodging of a document or formal statement (*libellus*) with the magistrate in charge of the court. Paulus (D. 48.2.3) provided the form of words required for the accusation of adultery, which included the consul and date; the name of the accuser, the name of the 'praetor or proconsul', and the name of the wife accused; the statute under which the accusation was brought; the nature of the accusation, including the name of the alleged lover (who was not the subject of the present accusation) and the exact place (the 'city of A' and the 'home of B') and the month of the occurrence of the alleged adultery. This clearly has features which applied only to the adultery charge, but suggests that, in *publica iudicia* cases, the statute would nor-mally be specified. The Lex Julia on *publica iudicia* set out the require-ments of place, person and month in general terms; if the legal form was not observed, the 'lodging of the name' (*delatio nominis*) was regarded as void and the accuser had to start again (D. 48.2.3.1 and 4).

The statute may also have covered questions of exemption from service as a juror or judge, or appearance as a witness, and the custody of slaves required to testify under torture. While the aim of the law was to stand-ardise and clarify procedure, its long-term effect was to 'codify' the *publica iudicia*. Ateius Capito's work on the public courts, which was part of a longer work on various matters, may have been a response to its appearance and have done no harm to his career (he was consul in AD 5). Like many such attempts at systematisation, the separate status of the *publica iudicia* as a 'closed' order of crimes would outlive its usefulness. As we shall see in the next chapter, specialist discussion of law and legal process found itself trapped between the requirements of an empire with an expanding citizen-ship and an increasingly irrelevant symbolic capital on the one hand, and on the other the terminologies and ways of thought imposed by the legal tradition.

FROM *QUAESTIO* TO *COGNITIO*

Many of the stages of a prosecution (or at least their rationale) could be transferred from the *quaestio* to the *cognitio* without undue disruption. Senatorial procedures in the first century also incorporated elements of the *quaestio* into their own hearings (Rivière 2002: 203–18) but, having the discretion to act as they wished, introduced variants too; an enquiry could be launched, for example, without the accused being summoned in person. The historians and other literary sources castigated the antics of the informers, especially senators such as Fulcinius Trio, suffect consul in 31 (Rutledge 2001: 234–5), who denounced their colleagues and were perceived as acting in their own interests rather than those of the collective. Even under the Republic, accusers had been regarded with suspicion, and speaking for the defence was held to be the more honourable occupation for the advocate (Cic. *Brutus* 130). Emperors too denounced the laying of anonymous accusations by informers. By the fourth century the term *delator*, informer, carried such negative connotations that respectable informants needed reassurance that they were not 'really' *delatores*; Constantine insisted that whoever denounced intrusive takers of auspices was not a *delator* but rather one deserving of reward (*CT* 9.16.1).

The *cognitio* shared with the *quaestio* the all-important requirement that a named accuser should be present and should pursue the case to its conclusion; in Acts of the Apostles, the governor, Felix, delays Paul's trial until his accusers arrive (23.35). The accuser was obliged to register his charge by a formal *subscriptio* or *inscriptio*, in which the details of the charge, the name of the accused and that of the accuser(s) were recorded. He had also to sign it personally or, if illiterate, ask a representative to do so on his behalf (D. 48.2.7.pr). Once the *libellus* of the *inscriptio* was lodged, there was no going back. If he abandoned it for any reason other than such unavoidable causes as the death of the person accused, he became liable to punishment under the Senatus Consultum Turpillianum (cf. D. 48.16), a decree which outlawed devices designed to fix the outcome of trials by exploiting legal loopholes and fixing prosecutions (Tac. *Ann.* 14.41). If he had signed the form of accusation (*inscriptio*) and then failed to show up for the main hearing, the case automatically collapsed and the accuser could find himself liable (D. 48.16.1.1) for a counter-charge of *calumnia*, 'asserting what was false', collusion with the defendant, that is, 'hiding the truth' (*praevaricatio*) or a failure, from personal motives, to persist with a public duty (*tergiversatio*).

In the trial of Apuleius, to be discussed below (chapter 9), the nominal prosecutor was a minor, who could not be liable for *calumnia*. A few decades after the trial Papinian addressed the abuse of accusations by putting up a front man, assimilating the practice to penalties under the SC Turpillianum (D. 48.16.13). He also advised that a judge might reject a prosecution's case, but not rule that the accusers were guilty of *calumnia*. The judge's decision was expressed in set forms of words: 'not proven' in effect acquitted of *calumnia*, while 'you have been guilty of *calumnia*' condemned (D. 48.16.4). In a brief rider to his original opinion Papinian stated that if a governor declared that 'this accusation was rashly brought', this also did not imply *calumnia* (D. 48.16.5).

Under Constantine and his successors, and in line with the general tightening of regulation in Late Antiquity, the discretion on *calumnia* accorded to governors down to the Severans was removed, and the failed accuser automatically incurred the penalty which had threatened the accused. This was well intentioned, in that one aim was to discourage frivolous prosecutions and ensure uniformity of penalty, but it made no allowance for the failure of cases which were in fact well founded, or for misunderstandings, superior power on one side and a possibly corrupt judge. The only resort was appeal to the emperor, who had power to vary sentences, and even undo the mistakes of his judges; thus in 384, for example, Symmachus (*Relatio* 49) petitioned for leniency for a worthy young man whose prosecution had failed (and who also happened to be a member of the imperial spy service). The precise nature of the punishment was discretionary, depending on the gravity of the offence; the principle also applied to cases brought *extra ordinem* (D. 48.16.3 and 15.1).

The confrontation between accuser and accused was a central principle of the functioning of public justice. Although at Rome advocates and their clients and supporters sat on benches at ground level, the visual confrontation was all-important for the drama of the occasion. Where governors are seen acting against wrongdoers without the presence of the accuser (for example in many cases of persecution of Christians), it can safely be assumed that they were acting in their role as keepers of the peace and general administrators of justice, a role for which no formal statutory sanction was required.

THE *QUAESTIO*-STATUTES UNDER THE EMPIRE

It is Augustus' statutes, mostly, rather than those of Caesar, which survived, as Leges Juliae, into the Later Empire, along with three Leges Corneliae, the Lex Fabia on kidnapping and the Lex Pompeia on parricide. However, they survived only in a limited, but significant, sense. The first defining feature to be lost was probably the procedural device of the *quaestio* itself. Under the Empire the statutes defined the *publica iudicia*, the public courts of judgement, which had initially been indeed the People's courts of early Rome. This redefinition resulted in a significant shift, or reversion, in meaning from 'investigation' (*quaestio*) to 'judgement' (*iudicium*). By Late Antiquity the word *quaestio* referred in a judicial context to investigation under torture, the Question (D. 48.18).

In so far as the texts of the *quaestio*-statutes can be known, they established procedures which could only be activated effectively at Rome. This, as we have seen, was certainly the case with the Gracchan law on extortion, which is the one *quaestio*-statute to survive virtually intact in epigraphic form. The same restrictions were still known to apply in the text of the Lex Cornelia on assassins and poisoners, as, in the reign of Caracalla, Ulpian was at pains to explain in his manual of instructions on the duties on the proconsul, or provincial governor (*Collatio* 1.3). The detailed provisions of the Latin Law of Irni in Baetica, dated to AD 91, and the longest extant text of the Vespasianic municipal charter (González 1986) show that there was a conscious effort, at least in the West, to assimilate local practices, where possible, to those current at Rome. But the application of this to the public criminal law was limited, as such cases fell under the jurisdiction of the governor's *cognitio*, which was expected to be locally responsive. Late in the first century the innovative jurist Proculus, in a general context, responded to worries about Rome-centredness by assuring provincial governors that they did not need to be bound by what happened at Rome (D. 1.18.12).

The Cyrene Edicts, from the reign of Augustus, show that there was some attempt, at least locally, to run jurisdiction involving Roman citizens through the use of juries. An album had been established, on the Roman pattern, from which the jurors were drawn. In response to local Greeks, who felt they were being discriminated against, Augustus raised the property qualification and insisted that Greeks be adlected onto the album and allowed half the places on the juries (*FIRA* 1.68, Edict 1). He also allowed the governor discretion as to whether he heard cases with his *consilium* or with the help of a panel of jurors (*FIRA* 1.68, Edict 4). A letter from Pliny shows that governors in Bithynia were still creating panels of judges early in the second century, although the exact purpose is unclear (Pliny, *Letter* 10.58.1).

The original distinctiveness of the *quaestio*-statutes was eroded over time in numerous ways. As we have seen, the offences covered reflected the priorities of a governing elite over a relatively short historical period. Under the Julio-Claudians, in the first century AD, their modification and the creation of new offences was controlled by the same elite, in the Senate, under the guidance of the emperor (Santalucia 1998: 205–13). Advocates were penalised for illegal behaviour in 20 and 47 under the SC Messalianum (Ulpian at *Collatio* 8.7.2 and Marcian at D. 48.10.1.1) and the SC Claudianum (Tac. *Ann.* 11.5–7). The Lex Cornelia on forgeries was extended in 27 and 29, under Tiberius, to perjurers and people who accepted bribes to make false accusations. These two *senatusconsulta*, the SC Licinianum (Ulpian at *Collatio* 8.7.1) and Geminianum (8.7.3) provide an interesting commentary on Tacitus' emphasis on the flurry of treason (and other) accusations under Tiberius; someone clearly thought it worth while to limit court abuses. Under Nero the Senate curtailed the outdated criminal jurisdiction of the tribunes through the SC Pisonianum, and accusers who tried to pull out of trials were fined and penalised with *infamia* (Tac. *Ann.* 14.41; D. 48.16; *CJ* 9.45). But as the independent powers of the Senate faded and its composition fell under the control of the emperors, some crimes fell into desuetude. *Ambitus*, electoral corruption, was one such, of which Modestinus observed that in the third century this offence was no longer of interest, as there were no longer any elections (D. 48.14.1.pr). However, the inclusion of *ambitus* in the Codes of Theodosius (9.26) and Justinian (9.26) shows the adaptability of old offences to new environments: *ambitus* could be treated as 'corruption', divorced from its electoral context and thus applied to the misdeeds of corrupt judges and official misdemeanours.

As new forms of law emanating from the emperor and his servants came to dominate in the courts, the texts of the statutes, which lacked the collective antiquarian authority of the Twelve Tables, seem to have been sidelined. It is unlikely that any complete texts of the Republican statutes were available to Late Antique commentators or judges. In court, where jurists could be cited as binding authorities, and in the imperial law offices they would have been superseded by later interpretations of individual clauses, by those authorised to make them. These interpretations reflected the legal attitudes and practices of their own day and therefore enabled discreet changes of emphasis from the original texts. Imperial constitutions were often issued in response to problems raised by governors as judges; these, along with senatorial decrees and juristic opinions, sometimes based on real cases, could explicitly modify the statute-tradition.

Unwary readers of the Digest chapters 'on' (*ad*) the Lex Cornelia or Lex Julia on X or Y must therefore be aware that what they read are interpretations of the statutes, not the statutes themselves. Over time, the social attitudes of the legislator could come to conflict with those of the legal interpreter sensitive to social change. A central principle of the Lex Julia on adulteries, for example, was that if a wife was suspected of adultery with a lover, it was incumbent on the husband to divorce and then prosecute, or he would himself be liable for prosecution and disgrace as a pimp (*leno*). This was contentious at the time and Tiberius was quick to retreat from Augustus' unwarranted intervention in family jurisdiction, by allowing the family council to act to discipline a woman suspected of adultery – provided that no public accusation had been brought by a third party (Suet. *Tib.* 35.1). Families, unlike the strict law, can forgive and by the third century Ulpian envisaged the possibility of reconciliation, advising parties in conflict over a wife's infidelity to remember that, morally, a husband should be faithful too and set a good example (D. 48.5.14(13).5; below, p. 100).

In fact, the collective identity of the *quaestio*-statutes was a retrospective creation due to their proximity to each other in time; to Augustus' law on the *publica iudicia*, probably passed in 17 BC (Bauman 1980); and their preservation as the framework for public law thereafter. The *ad hoc* nature of their creation meant that, as a collection, they lacked cohesion. For example, the *quaestio*-statutes did not all entail a capital penalty. The extortion laws required restitution of the moneys extorted and a multiple of the sum assessed as the penal element (*RS* I, 91, lines 58–9). Writing in the late second or early third century on the Praetor's Edict, the jurist Paulus observed that, of the *publica iudicia*, some would impose a capital penalty, meaning death, exile and loss of civil rights, while other penalties were financial, in the shape of a fine, or corporal punishment (D. 48.1.2).

The statutes' distinctiveness was further eroded by changes in penal practice, usually in the direction of greater judicial severity (Garnsey 1968; MacMullen 1986). These were furthered by the evolution of two new legal categories of person, based on social status (Garnsey 1970), the *honestiores* (more honourable) and the *humiliores* (more humble, lit. closer to the ground). Marcian's handbook on Roman law, the *Institutes*, explained that the penalty specified by the Lex Cornelia on assassins and poisoners was deportation to an island and confiscation of all possessions (D. 48.8.3.5). However, 'today', the custom was to throw lower-class homicides to the wild beasts in the arena, while those of higher station were deported to an island. This would still be described by the legal interpreters in the third century as 'the penalty of the Lex Cornelia', despite its divergence from the actual content of the statute; what the jargon meant was 'conviction under' the Lex Cornelia, not the specific penalty envisaged by Sulla.

Despite the processes of modification, and their failure to preserve a distinct procedural and penal identity, the *quaestio*-statutes proved remarkably durable. This was in part because of their antiquity; continuity with the past reinforced the authority of the legal tradition against competing pressures, not least from emperors whose legal grasp, from the third century onwards, was open to question (for Valentinian I and treason, see Matthews 1989: 209–18). But they were also accepted, both by the imperial administration and by Romans in the provinces, as a useful means of identifying a 'public offence', which enabled prosecutions to be brought by any concerned citizen (Just. *Inst.* 4.18.1). These 'accusations' were subject to formal subscription, or inscription, which, as stated in the fourth-century Edict on Accusations (*FIRA* 1.459–60, lines 10–23), made the accuser liable to the 'severe' penalty which threatened the defendant. The process of inscription was intended to deter malicious or unfounded accusations, although, given an apparent preference on the part of some for the criminal route (D. 47.12.8 and 13.1–2, see on Macer below), the extent of the deterrent effect is uncertain.

As mentioned above (p. 17), the choice of offences to be classified as 'public' by the *quaestio*-statutes was essentially arbitrary, and by the third century the strains were beginning to show. A jurist called Aemilius Macer wrote a treatise on the *publica iudicia*, which he probably began by seeking to explain the inconsistencies resulting from the survival of the *quaestio* categories, which were clearly now perceived by some as anachronistic (D. 48.1.1):

Not all the courts of judgement, in which an accusation (*crimen*) may be brought, are also public but only those which derive from the statutes on public courts, for example the Lex Julia on *maiestas* (etc.)

Macer also, like Paulus, had difficulties with penalties. The penalty of loss of civil rights known as *infamia* resulted not from every accusation brought but only from those heard before a *publicum iudicium* (D. 48.1.7). But, as he must quickly have realised, *infamia* could also be imposed by a 'private court', such as those which judged theft, robbery with violence and outrage (*iniuria*).

It is sometimes assumed that legal change must have been driven by the elite who, as members of the various interest groups who contributed to the constituent parts of Roman law, would have controlled its content. Certainly, as we shall see, much of public criminal law did not apply to the poorer and less reputable sections of the population, who, in Constantine's words, were 'not considered worthy of notice by the laws' (*CT* 9.7.1, of 326). Moreover, a certain level of economic power and social status must be assumed for anyone able to bring an action at all.

But advice offered to litigants by Macer's handbook suggests that his readership were interested in legal dodges, which could be exploited to expand the remit of the *publica iudicia*, and that this readership would have consisted of litigants, rather than law-makers. Extortion with menaces (*concussio*), for example, was not formally a public offence. However, if money was handed over to someone to avert the threat of prosecution, it was possible to resort to the *publicum iudicium* procedure on the grounds that the Lex Cornelia on homicide had been interpreted by senatorial decree as applying to those who threatened an accusation against the innocent, or who accepted money for bringing or not bringing an accusation, or acting or not acting as a witness (D. 47.13.1–2). Macer also believed that the Lex Julia on public violence, which proscribed interfering with burial or entombment, could be deployed in cases of tomb violation, as this could be construed as interference with the corpse (D. 47.12.8).

The legal tradition, as expressed in the survival of the *quaestio*-statutes as *publica iudicia*, was therefore under pressure from many sides. Not all of it was deliberate manipulation by interested parties. The expansion of the Roman citizenship in particular had judicial consequences, the extent of which is open to debate (Garnsey 2004: 140–9). The advent of imperial rule encouraged the superseding of the *quaestio* procedure by hearings before either the Senate or a single judge in Rome or the provinces. The original statutory definitions of offences were changed and modified over time, encouraged by the flexibility of the *cognitio* procedure. The penalties of the law, where specified, were not sacrosanct and were altered by judicial practice. The use of appeal from sentence (*appellatio*) increased, along with its regulation. And legal advisers acted in concert with aggrieved litigants to expand the application of public criminal procedures.

CHAPTER 3

Cognitio

COGNITIO

The powers of governors over Roman citizens abroad was extensive, although the precise extent is unclear. In some cases, such as Galba's crucifixion of a citizen in Spain (Suet. *Galba* 9.1) or the condemnation of Fl. Archippus of Bithynia to the mines in *c.* AD 84 (Pliny, *Letter* 10. 58), the governor's power over citizens in the provinces appears to have been absolute. But Roman citizens abroad, threatened with conviction on capital charges, also seem to have had the right of having their cases transferred to Rome, if the governor saw fit; Paul of Tarsus employed this device, partly perhaps in order to escape the social pressures exerted by his enemies and their supporters (Acts 25.1–12). As the citizenship expanded, this form of appeal (*provocatio*) appears to have become less viable. Instead, those convicted or dissatisfied with the outcome in a lesser court would resort to appeal against the judge's decision (*appellatio*; see D. 49.1–13; *CT* 11.29–38).

Governors heard cases not as presidents of *quaestiones* but as individual judges, sitting on their public tribunals and backed by an advisory council of distinguished friends and legal advisors. If a governor and the litigants' legal representatives were doing their job efficiently (and had access to Roman archives or equivalent provincial collections), the governor might have had resort to a melange of different legal sources to help his decision. An illustration from the second century is the miscellaneous collection assembled by the Roman jurist Venuleius Saturninus to inform his discussion of which types of person were liable (or not) to be accused (D. 48.2.12). His documentation included a 'resolution of Lentulus' passed in 31; a letter of Hadrian to the consul Glabrio (124); the Lex Julia on *publica iudicia* (not necessarily at first hand); a senatorial resolution from 20; the Lex Julia on private violence; and the Lex Pompeia on parricide. But many, if not most, governors would have been content with less.

The exact scope of governors' powers may always have been uncertain, because they could be defined in different ways. The holding of *imperium*, the right to give orders, allowed discretion to magistrates to do what was required to preserve the peace (Greenidge 1901/1971: 331–8; Lintott 1999a: 97–9, 226–8; Nippel 1995: 5–12). There was a list of especially heinous offences, supplied by Ulpian for the benefit of governors – kidnapping, banditry, theft and sacrilege (D. 1.18.13) – which the governor could pursue by actively 'hunting down' the perpetrators, thus keeping the province free from 'bad men'. This list bears only an incidental relationship to the offences proscribed by the statutes; theft was not a public offence in a statutory sense, in that it had no *quaestio*-statute, and banditry was always a policing matter, for which no statute was deemed necessary. However, juristic discourse also provided guidance on how the definitions of offences and the penalties of the *quaestio*-statutes could be applied in a provincial context, providing continuity with the legal tradition of the *publica iudicia*. As we shall see, with reference to Apuleius' trial in Africa in the late 150s AD, the extent to which the governors needed to bother with references to a historical statutory framework is not at all clear (below, chapter 9).

Following on the juristic practice of referring to the hearing of certain civil and criminal cases as *extra ordinem* (outside the legal framework), modern scholarship has made much of the so-called *cognitio extra ordinem*. I have suggested above (p. 9), that this is specialist vocabulary, and that its transfer to modern analysis may be unhelpful (see also Orestano 1980). The term has been used in at least two senses by moderns, one to refer to the process of *cognitio* itself (Buti 1982; Tellegen-Couperus 1993: 90), the second (favoured by the present author) to hearings of accusations not covered by existing statutes or other forms of positive law and legal interpretation. The device can also be referred to as *cognitio extraordinaria*, as it is in the Digest heading (47.11), relating to a selection of cases not covered by any *ordo*, as conceived by the juristic tradition. The difficulty with the term, for the layman, is that it implies that such proceedings were perceived not only by jurists but also by non-specialists as being somehow 'extraordinary' or exceptional, rather than being the outcome of evolutionary processes of legal change, which were assisted by the flexibility of the *cognitio* process.

On the first view, because the *cognitio* differed from the two-stage process used at Rome, it was in that sense 'extra-ordinary'; this reading is consistent with juristic tendencies to use Rome as a procedural reference point, despite the risks of anachronism, but is unhelpful for modern analysis. In civil cases the *ordo*, therefore, was determined to a great extent by what the praetor did. In the first stage of the civil process at Rome the magistrate established the legal point at issue and appointed a judge or panel to determine the facts of the case; in the second, the judge(s) heard and adjudicated on the facts and associated legal points (see briefly, Lintott 2004: 64–8).

But if this was the meaning of the *ordo* – that it was the procedural 'order' of things at Rome – it was divorced from the experience of all outside the City. It was Rome-centred and, as the citizenship expanded throughout the provinces, increasingly irrelevant in practice. Even under the Republic, from the standpoint of provincials in the provinces the *cognitio* process was the way that Roman jurisdiction was seen to operate. True, there was a cultural connection with Rome because, under the Late Republic, pro-praetors and pro-consuls already had extensive experience of the operation of law at Rome. In their Provincial Edicts, therefore, they laid out how they would operate the law, usually in the Roman terms with which they were familiar (Richardson 1983).

In the *cognitio* the two stages observed at Rome could be merged into one, although in civil cases the governor did have extensive powers of delegation, partly to ease his workload (D. 1.21). This also enabled the governor to give decisions on matters not formally covered by civil, praetorian or public criminal law. It was these hearings which were 'extra-ordinary', but they were not 'extraordinary' in the sense of being 'exceptional'. In terms of process, the governor in his *cognitio* could introduce his own variants. This allowed the jurisdictional system to respond more quickly to new demands made upon it. Cases brought *extra ordinem*, in the second sense, represented a useful means of expanding legal remedies by a creative use of magisterial discretion, backed, where necessary, by imperial endorsement. For example, under praetorian law, a man who carried out a mandate and spent money but was denied a refund by the mandator could sue under the action for mandate (*actio mandati*). However, if, in addition, he had been promised some kind of payment for his services, so-called 'salt-money' (*salarium*), a rescript of Severus and Caracalla (*CJ* 4.35.1; R. Zimmerman 1996: 416) declared that he could sue for that before the provincial governor, or *praeses*. Another new offence, admitted by Marcus Aurelius as an 'accusation' to be pursued *extra ordinem* was the plundering or despoiling of an inheritance (D. 47.19.1). As these adaptations continued, so also they accumulated to the point where they could not possibly be regarded, in practice, as exceptional or 'extraordinary'. Yet the innate conservatism of legal discourse continued to categorise sensible innovations as requiring to be heard *extra ordinem*, even though non-specialists, especially in Late Antiquity, would have had little or no idea what the *ordo* was.

The same developments occurred in public trials. Aemilius Macer was asked if the SC Turpillianum, on false accusations, applied to public cases heard *extra ordinem*; he replied (D. 48.16.15.1) that emperors had ruled that they should be decided on a case by case basis, which was wise, given that a case could fail for reasons of incompetence, collusion or social pressures, as well as malice. Ulpian's general view on governors who were required to decide punishments in cases brought *extra ordinem* was that they could err a little on the side of leniency or severity, but not too much (D. 48.19.13); he also allowed those who were required to pay for their offence with money but were too poor to do so to be subjected to special measures by the judge (D. 48.19.1.3). This formal recognition of discretion in *extra ordinem* cases had a significant impact on the system overall. The 'judicial severity' of Late Antiquity identified by Ramsay MacMullen (1986) and others was precisely that – severity on the part of judges, not (necessarily) the emperor.

The evolution of trials *extra ordinem* was also driven by litigants, especially accusers. It was they, not the governors, who tested the system, to see what 'crimes' were admissible for trial by the Roman authorities. Luke's depiction in the Acts of the Apostles of Paul's difficulties with his enemies illustrates the opportunism of accusers and the reluctance of the Roman authorities to become embroiled in local squabbles (Sherwin White 1963: 48–70). Paul is confronted by his accusers, who allege mis-behaviour in the Temple and stirring up discord among Jews 'everywhere' (Acts 24.5). They must have hoped to be taken seriously because of the public-order implications. Instead, the charges are rejected as being outside the competence of the Roman judges (Acts 23.19 and 25.18–19) but 'kept on file' to avoid complaints later. Paul, in the meantime, successfully applies to have his case transferred to Rome.

Much confusion, then and now, might have been avoided, had jurists been prepared to jettison the increasingly anachronistic *ordo* of 'public' and other offences. Instead, the system adjusted itself by adding new offences 'outside' the *ordo*. One example is the legal response to the infinite ingenuity of tricksters. Papinian, under Severus, admitted that the process for *stellionatus* (swindling) was 'neither public nor private' (D. 47.20.1). Ulpian's advice to the 'proconsul' (D. 47.20.3) was that *stellionatus* could be used as a catch-all for any kind of fraud not covered by statute. Having listed a few examples, such as dishonestly disposing of a pledged article or collusion to the detriment of another, Ulpian appears to lose interest, only to add one further example as an afterthought (D. 47.20.3.3); his real point was that a list was unnecessary and restrictive. The penalty too had to be fixed *extra ordinem*: at worst this entailed a sentence to the mines for people of lower status, and for *honestiores* temporary exile or loss of civic status.

Ulpian's contemporary Callistratus broke ranks with tradition, writing not on *publica iudicia* but specifically on *cognitiones*. This can be seen as an attempt to revise the old categories in order to reflect the realities of contemporary judicial practice. The name Callistratus is Greek in origin, and he does not appear to be part of the charmed circle of imperial jurists. However, the facts that he wrote in Latin, and about Roman law, and that his work survived point to his being not entirely without connections or influence. Certainly, whatever his place of origin, Callistratus perceived himself as Roman in culture. His treatise on public legal hearings divided *cognitiones* into four categories (D. 50.13.5): the conduct of magistracies (*honores*) and public liturgies (*munera*); cases involving money; cases involving reputation (*existimatio*); and accusations of capital crimes. If an attempt is made to analyse these in terms of the historical categories, problems immediately arise. The notion of the accusation, *crimen*, is defined in terms of its being 'capital', not in terms of its antecedents as 'public'; the putting of 'reputation' into a separate category is odd, because many charges combined *infamia*, or loss of reputation, with either financial or personal punishment; and the holding of administrators to account was never a separate legal category. Yet, Callistratus' 'categories' may echo other attempts at alternative systems, based on *existimatio*. Cicero, for example, in the *Pro Caecina* (69 BC) distinguished two kinds of civil actions, the first merely pecuniary and the second, more seriously, threatening damage to 'reputation' for the loser (*Caec.* 2.6–4.10). Callistratus' analysis reflects some independence of thought, perhaps the result of his non-governmental perspective, and a recognition of the consequences for the legal tradition of the now virtually universal operation of the *cognitio*, which responded not to outdated categories but to perceived contemporary needs.

Through the flexibility of the *cognitio* process, law developed in response to the needs of litigants. Its operation in terms of both offences and penalties was shaped not only by the jurists but also by the attitudes of judges, some perhaps more aware of politics or mass opinion than the law, and of the emperors, to whom the governors referred for endorsement and advice on their decisions. Over five hundred years passed from the death of Augustus, the last author of statutes on *publica iudicia*, in AD 14 to the codification of the *ius civile* by Justinian in the 530s. In that period, juristic discourse and imperial attempts to impose system on competing forms of legal enactment either assimilated new offences to ancient statutes or labelled them as 'extraordinary'. But the judges 'on the ground' were not primarily concerned with the niceties of the ancient statutes – provided that they understood when an accuser from the 'public' was required for a case to be brought. In their courts the skills of advocates and legal advisers, the standing of litigants and their supporters, and the will of the crowd and the prejudices of the judges had as much bearing on the fates of the accused as did the letter of the law.

TORTURE AND SOCIAL STATUS

First impressions of rules on the mandatory torture of slaves who were required to give evidence suggest that the Romans had no problems in accepting the 'application of pain' (D. 48.18.1, *tormenta*) in a judicial context. Whereas today torture of any kind and in any context is forbidden under international law (although there are limitations in practice on enforcement), the Romans appear at ease with its use in their system. By Late Antiquity interrogation under torture was not confined to slaves but had extended, probably through court practice, to the lower classes of freemen and women (Robinson 2006: ch. 5). Clearly judges found the Question useful, perhaps (if Christian martyr-acts are to be believed) even congenial.

In fact attitudes were more complex. Modern views of torture might not distinguish between the infliction of pain in the course of interrogation and the suffering caused by certain forms of execution, such as crucifixion, which might now be defined as 'terroristic torture', the infliction of pain to deter others. The Romans, however, were clear that there was such a distinction. Judicial torture by definition should not end in the death of the victim (although it sometimes did), as this would contradict the aim of the process, which was to establish the truth. Nor should a person be executed by torture (or flogging or scourging, D. 48.19.8.3). When they considered pain in the context of punishment, this was to do with the function of punishment as deterrent or as an affirmation of the power of the state over the body of the criminal.

The starting point of the Roman willingness to torture slaves for evidence was the fact that the victims were slaves, a form of property, and therefore not eligible for the rights accorded free people. An accused slave, against whom there was other evidence (D. 48.18.1.1), could well be subjected to *tormenta* to force a confession; even if he held out, he might still be condemned (Val. Max. 8.4.2). Of course, there is extensive evidence for the fact that in real life many Romans (though not all) respected the humanity of their slaves, who might be freed at some point and themselves attain the rights and protections of citizenship. But the accepted use of torture of slaves, which, having been established, was never questioned, had an unintended consequence. Once judicial torture was 'legalised' in one limited respect, it became possible to extend its use, hence the increased risk of the infliction of judicial savagery on free people in Late Antiquity (MacMullen 1986). In one case under Constantine a decurion, in theory exempt from torture, produced suspect answers under interrogation and was taken away to be subjected later to 'more severe questioning' (Optatus, *Against the Donatists*, Appendix 2.10).

There was a further complication which allowed the extension of torture in trials. The rule that anyone, except senators, was liable to judicial torture in cases of *maiestas* allowed a further extension of the practice, as a number of crimes, such as counterfeiting coinage or the use of purple dye, became assimilated to treason. Because of the two definitions of treason, an offence against the emperor or an offence against public security (see below, chapter 6), the original rationale of the convention was obscured. If the latter, and far more ancient, definition, public safety, is used, then it becomes clear why the civil rights of free individuals were subordinated to the security of the community. As ever, the *salus populi* was the supreme law.

In less serious cases the Romans did not rush to judgement. Even where slaves were concerned, emperors believed that the courts should show restraint. Augustus stipulated that torture should not be used as a device of first resort; the hearing of other evidence by the court was required in order to establish if there was a case to answer (D. 48.18.1.pr.). Moreover, it was widely acknowledged, even by legal writers, that as a device for ascertaining the truth it was unreliable; those tortured might be strong enough to hold out, say what was expected or, if hostile to the accused, try to incriminate him (D. 48.18.1.23). For this reason the Romans operated the rule of corroboration: an accused person could not be condemned on the basis of torture evidence alone.

Views on the use (and abuse) of torture as a means of interrogation were mixed. As a former advocate, Quintilian was well qualified to argue both sides of the torture issue. One view, he wrote (*Inst.* 5.4), was that torture made admission of the truth inevitable. The other was that it resulted in false statements, either because the victim was tough and could persuade the torturers that his/her lies were truth, or because he/she was weak and told lies because that was what was wanted. Quintilian's view seems to have been that evidence under torture could itself be disputed. The advocate could ask who had asked for torture to be used or had offered a particular witness; against whom was the evidence given? Why had the victim been requested or volunteered? More questions could be asked about the process itself: who was in charge of the torture? What were the methods used and against whom? Was the evidence extracted credible or consistent? Did the victim persist in his (her) initial statement or change it, because of the pain? Did the change happen at the start or as the torture progressed? Quintilian's questions may also shed light on why the use of torture persisted, despite doubts as to the veracity of the evidence produced. Whatever the counter-arguments, the presence of pain allowed an extra dimension to the evidence and to the disputes of advocates about it.

It should also be noted in passing here that, under all procedures, the use of torture on Christians appears to be anomalous. The aim was not to extract information, as Christian martyrs were (allegedly) all eager to announce themselves guilty as charged. While some degree of exaggeration in the sources, especially the lurid accounts of Eusebius, may be allowed for, the process appears to have sought to achieve public recantation on the Christian's part, which would be evidenced by their offering sacrifice or incense to the emperor and cursing Christ. This was not, therefore, intended to be torture as punishment, or execution by torture, although it could amount to the same thing, but the creation of a different kind of 'example', the undermining and splitting of the Christian community by the forcible creation of apostates. The martyr accounts emphasise the tortures to under-line the message about the courage of their witness. That purpose may well obscure the real techniques and aims of the authorities.

PUNISHMENT IN THEORY AND PRACTICE

Had Apuleius (see below, chapter 9, pp. 123–7), who was tried for magic, been condemned under the Lex Cornelia, he would not have faced the penalty stated in the original statute: interdiction from fire and water had been superseded by exile. If a really serious view had been taken of his nocturnal sacrifices, he, as a member of the Roman citizen elite, would not have faced the unpleasant and degrading treatment meted out to the lower classes; the worst he could fear was decapitation, but permanent exile, with loss of civil rights (deportation), was the most likely option.

Under the Republic Romans were remarkably reluctant to impose the death penalty on their fellow-citizens for anything but the most serious offences, even after a trial. The favoured punishment was the expulsion of the offender from the community through 'interdiction from fire and water'. The criminal became an exile, a man without a state. For lesser, financial or non-public misdemeanours, offenders suffered fines, legal disabilities or physical chastisement on the order of a magistrate. Later, wrote Ulpian of his own day (D. 48.19.2.1), interdiction was replaced by deportation to an island, which, although a form of internal exile combined with loss of citizen rights, lacked the quasi-religious tone of a sentence excluding the criminal from the necessities of life.

Under the Empire, as we have seen, status through citizenship was gradually replaced by a new social hierarchy. People were categorised as *honestior* – with the status of a decurion or better – or as lowly *humilior*. The rich criminal always fared better than his 'humble' counterpart, not only because he had a better chance of manipulating the result of his trial through connections and patronage, but also because respect for status extended to protection even of the guilty from the humiliations inflicted on inferior people. Thus, while the convicted *honestior* faced execution by beheading, the *humilior* might be burned alive, crucified or thrown to the wild beasts. In the latter case he might have to wait for a while in prison minus his civil rights, which were already forfeit, until the time of the next public games. The equivalent of relegation or deportation to an island for the *honestior* was, for the *humilior*, a period of servitude in the mines, perhaps for a fixed term, perhaps for life. Men of higher rank were also not to be beaten with rods but to have 'the same honour as decurions' (D. 48.19.28.5).

Sentencing to the mines could be read as shrewd economics: a workforce was supplied cheaply and was easily renewed. But considerations of honour, status and respect mattered more, and the thinking behind sentencing to the mines (as also to the beasts in the arena) was not economic but social (Millar 1984). Punishments for people of lower status were physically humiliating as well as painful. Suffering in the mines was less visible, but still profoundly degrading. In the arena the executions of criminals, including bandits, were public and often prolonged and bizarre, sometimes with mythological themes attached (Coleman 1990). One bandit, Laureolus, was both crucified and eaten by a 'Caledonian' bear ('Martial', *Liber Spectaculorum* 7). And in Carthage in 203 Christian martyrs were compelled to enter the arena dressed gaudily as priests of Saturn and priestesses of Ceres (*Passion of Perpetua and Felicitas* 18.4–5).

Sentencing evolved under the Empire through judicial practice, endorsed, or not, by imperial sanction. Repeatedly, the legal commentators observe that a sentencing practice was 'accepted' or 'generally agreed' or 'customary' (e.g. D. 48.19.1.pr; 1.3; 2.1; 3; 8.8; 8.10; 8.12; 9.pr; 9.4–7; 9.10–11; and so on). On the question of whether a governor should punish delinquent slaves or leave them to his successor, 'many precedents' supported the former course of action (D. 48.19.6.1). From this we might conclude that governors had total discretion in sentencing and that the citizen and subject had little protection from the arbitrary exercise of gubernatorial power. However, custom worked both ways. There appears to have been some kind of tariff of sentences for some of the statutory crimes, and in cases heard (and punished) *extra ordinem* judges had discretion either way from an assumed norm, but 'not beyond what is reasonable' (Ulpian, at D. 48.19.13 in the context of appeals); the line from which the variations were to be measured is not specified but would be established by analogy with comparable crimes – and the assumptions of the governor about what was appropriate. And although rules restricting the use of torture and other forms of physical indignity were eroded over time, they still provided some protection, as well as ground for appeal, for those who could afford it.

What was punishment for? The ever-helpful Aulus Gellius, whose combination of curiosity with lack of originality makes him an invaluable witness for Roman social attitudes in the mid second century, wrote that punishment had three functions: to reform and correct, especially when someone had done wrong by accident or chance, as he would be made more careful in future (*NA* 7.14.2); second, the need to prevent loss of face on the part of the victim, again a limited reason (7.14.3); and finally, and most important, to act as an example, as the fear of a ferocious penalty will deter others. Gellius observed that the first and third functions were also endorsed by Plato; in a discussion on the Twelve Tables (*NA* 20.1, below, pp. 55–7) he approved Caecilius' opinion that bad people of old were so intimidated by the penalties laid down that they avoided doing wrong, and therefore the penalties were never used. Caecilius' view would have been shared by Callistratus, who wrote of the suspension of robbers on gibbets that it was done at the scenes of their crimes to act as a deterrent to others, and to gratify their victims (D. 48.19.28.15).

Aulus Gellius did not include retribution in his list of functions. However, 'revenge' featured prominently in the language of punishment in Late Antiquity and was probably a motive earlier. One feature of juristic advice on options for litigants, as we have seen, is the preference shown either by them or by their clients for the 'public' route, which would give them not the pecuniary compensation of the civil charge but 'revenge' in the shape of the punishment of the offender. On occasion, the reason may simply have been that pecuniary restitution was not possible: the poor thief had spent his illicit gains already. But it may also be suggested that the expanding use of the public route and of what MacMullen (1986) termed 'judicial savagery' was driven not (only) by the emperors but by litigants and by the courts.

JUDICIAL INCOMPETENCE

Governors acting as judges made mistakes. We know of those that were picked up on appeal, but not those acts of injustice that were never reported; judicial error is therefore probably under-reported in the sources. Moreover, because the contexts are often challenges to excessive severity, the errors all appear to tend in one direction – that governors, because of ignorance or in response to the culture of their time, were harsher than the law allowed. For example, under Severus, a slave was handed over by a judge 'by mistake' to forced labour, which was unlawful (D. 48.19.34). People were not supposed to be executed by torture, but it would be hard to differentiate between that and death under torture, which, as the jurists acknowledged, did take place, and which was frequently attested in Christian martyrdoms. A judge passing a sentence of servitude in the mines might 'forget' because of incompetence (*imperitia*) to impose a time limit; in such a case, the sentence was to last for ten years (Modestinus, at D. 48.19.23). Implementation of sentence once passed generated further failures in the system. Pliny the Younger, dispatched by Trajan to clean up Bithynia in the early second century, found people sentenced to the mines and the arena cheerfully working as public slaves (*Letters* 10.31 and 32); sentences of banishment passed by previous governors were either not enforced or reversed without proper documentation (10.56 and 57); and an alleged forger condemned to the mines continued to practise his trade as a philosopher, his dubious position apparently secured by a character reference from the emperor Domitian (10.58–60).

Both jurists and emperors had cause to complain. Ulpian, who worked in the central administration, complained bitterly of the stupidity, wrong-headedness and folly of a judge in a civil case (D. 21.2.51.pr.) and acknowledged the ignorance of some in criminal hearings too (D. 49.1.1). Governors were not supposed to use prison as a punishment but they regularly did so (D. 48.19.8.9). Essential procedures were sometimes ignored. In the mid third century Gordian III objected when a governor condemned a man to the mines in his absence even though he had not been charged with anything (*CJ* 9.2.6, of 243); and in the 290s a governor had his sentence against one Zoilus annulled, because he had not delivered it in public (*CJ* 7.45.6, of 283).

In one juristic example of procedural malpractice, which refers to a real case involving an imperial decision made on appeal, a man, whose wife had died, claimed that she had lent money to one Surus and demanded its return (D. 48.18.20). He produced one witness, the son of his freedman, and demanded that Surus' slave girl be tortured. Surus objected that, first, he did not have the money, second, the unsupported testimony of one witness was not admissible and, third, it was not the custom to begin an investigation with torture (a custom which was laid down by Augustus and by Hadrian, see D. 48.18.1.pr.). The emperor upheld the appeal on the points of the single witness and the use of torture. What is significant here for the incompetence of judges is that the two principles apparently unknown to this *iudex* were both basic to the proper administration of justice.

In this context, issues raised by Christian writers as to the lawfulness of governors' treatment of suspected Christians should come as no surprise. There was some official confusion about why they were liable to be punished, although there was no doubt that they should be. The core objection, as the correspondence between Trajan and Pliny makes clear (Pliny, *Letters* 10.96–7), was the 'name of Christian' (*nomen Christianum*): if the accused made sacrifice to the emperor, (s)he could not be a Christian and was therefore released. But Pliny had also investigated more concrete charges of 'unspeakable practices' (*flagitia*), for which no evidence was found. In this case, for lack of evidence of other forms of wrongdoing, the Roman authorities appear to be persecuting the 'belief' in its own right; however, the insistence on sacrifice suggests that the real concern was with the perceived 'atheism' of the Christians, which could be read as both offensive to the tutelary deities of Rome and treasonable towards the emperors. Moreover, Trajan's practice was consistent with the emphasis on externals as evidence of belief; the governor of Africa who interviewed Cyprian, the bishop of Carthage, in 257, referred to the edict of Valerian and Gallienus which ordered that 'those who do not celebrate the religion of the Romans are obliged to recognise the Romans' rites' (*Acts of Cyprian* 1.1). 'The question of believing was seldom made explicit but the question of performing correctly was ever present' (Momigliano 1986: 107).

Accounts of Christian persecution confirm what has been argued above, that governors had extensive discretion as to how they observed or created the rules. Worry about the legal process prompted the letter of Serennius Granianus to Hadrian (Justin, *Apology* 1.68 = (in Greek) Eusebius, *Church History* 4.8.6–7), which objected to failures of procedure, insisting that Christians should have a proper trial and not be subjected to mob justice.

Hadrian's reply, to Granianus' successor, Minucius Fundanus (Justin, *Apology* 1.68 = Eus. *Church History* 4.9), admitted the existence of a problem. Christians should be made to answer before the tribunal, and the governor should not be influenced by rumours or the clamour of the crowd. Rather, a formal accusation should be lodged, the governor should decide if the accused had broken the law, and if the accuser had engaged in *calumnia* he should be punished accordingly. While the nature of the charge is left vague, the focus of imperial concern is clear: Christians should be subject to the same trial procedures (and safeguards) as everyone else.

Such was not the case at Lyon in 177, in the reign of Marcus Aurelius. There, according to the eyewitness account written by the local Christians, the governor, unsure of his ground but desperate to appease the mob, persistently violates not only natural justice but also the previous enactments of emperors. The persecution of the Christians of Lyon and Vienne is initiated by the local authorities and the mob, who first ban the Christians from all public spaces, then drag them into the Forum, subject them to interrogation and imprison them, pending the arrival of the governor (Eus. *Church History* 5.1.7–8). When the governor first hears the case (with the local authorities presumably acting as prosecutors), his hostility is obvious, evoking a protest against his 'unreasonable judgement' from an onlooker, who is arrested as a Christian in his turn (5.1.10).

But what was the offence? Torture is used on a number of Christians (although interrogation of the free under torture was unlawful) to extract confessions not of 'being Christian', which all the faithful freely admit, but of cannibalism and incest (5.1.17–20), encouraged by the earlier 'confessions' of two pagan slaves. One victim, an apostate, promptly reconverts and denies the charge of cannibalism, pointing out that Christians were vegetarians (5.1.25–6). Contrary to Trajan's ruling that those who recanted should be let off, the governor convicts the apostates, as 'murderers and committers of sacrilege', while charging the steadfast Christians with the lesser offence of 'being Christian' (5.1.32–5).

His attitude to punishment was equally cavalier. Most confessed Lyon Christians were strangled in prison or died of the conditions there (5.1.27–8) – neither course is justified in penal law, which insisted on public punishment, denied the right of the 'noose' (as opposed to public hanging) to governors (D. 48.19.8.1) and forbade prison as a punishment (48.19.8.9). In a brief return to legality, the governor refuses, temporarily, the public execution of a Roman citizen, Attalus, pending the arrival of a letter from the emperor instructing him what to do (Eus. *Church History* 5.1.43–4). When the letter arrives, policy changes dramatically. Christians who recanted were not to be accused of other things but let go (5.1.47–8), in line with previous imperial rulings. The governor may also have been reminded (briefly) of penal policy; correctly, he beheads the Roman citizens and sends the others to the arena, although the citizen Attalus is added to their number because he was a special hate-figure for the mob. Then, in a further reversion to crowd-pleasing, he instructs the public torture in the arena of several Christians. Death by torture was officially forbidden (D. 48.19.8.3), but judicial practice in the supply of criminals and outlaws to the games provided effective legal cover.

The Lyon governor was to have a long and inglorious line of literary and historical successors, whose inhumanity and lack of self-control further enhanced the glories of the martyrs and generated a new form of literature (Harries 1999). What is significant about this narrative is the extent of the legal misbehaviour indulged in by the governor without, apparently, much fear of being held to account. It was understandable that he was uncertain of the grounds for punishing Christians, and he was not alone in pandering to the mob. But, if the account can be trusted on this, the governor dealt directly with the accused without the use of formal accusations, resorted to torture of free people as well as slaves to extract confessions, failed to release those Christians who recanted until reminded (or informed) of policy by the emperor, and combined sentencing to the beasts with further tortures in the arena itself.

CONCLUSION

The Roman public criminal system is often criticised for its harshness and, in later years, for its corruption and exploitation of terror. By modern standards these criticisms are at least partly justified. But the attention paid by the authors of the early statutes to the stages of the process and the requirement that every move be tested by magistrate or by a jury panel suggests that, at least under the Republic, accusations were not lightly admitted. Moreover, a failed accusation could automatically trigger a counter-suit of *calumnia* and in Late Antiquity the accuser could face the same penalty as the defendant in the event of failure. This may have made redress less accessible to those without influence or patrons to turn to – and it did not solve the problem of bribery of juries – but it also deterred, to some extent, the frivolous prosecution.

Moreover, throughout Antiquity there was a consistent emphasis on the public operation of Roman justice. While some hearings did occur in private 'behind the curtain', the general practice was for the praetor at

Rome or the provincial governor to sit visibly above the crowd, his every word and gesture a matter of scrutiny by a critical public (see *CT* 1.16.6–7, of 331). If he engaged in judicial malpractice or was simply incompetent, he would be held to account by the interested parties; Libanius of Antioch, for example, castigated the slow pace of justice under the governor of Syria, Tisamenos, in 386, expecting the emperor to take note (*Oration* 33.9). This culture of complaint made governors more accountable, at least to those with the education and connections to voice complaints and make them stick, but it did little for the image of the workings of Roman justice.

CHAPTER 4

The thief in the night

The streets of Rome at night were unlit and dangerous for travellers. One night, a wayfarer, carrying a leaded whip perhaps for self-protection, picks up a torch from a shop fronting the street. The owner sees him, gives chase and seizes him by the arm. The traveller retaliates with his whip, a fight breaks out and the traveller is blinded in one eye. The traveller then sues the shopkeeper (Alfenus, Digest at D. 9.8.52.1). The opinion of the learned expert was that the outcome of the case would depend on the answer to the question of fact: who had started the brawl?

This imaginary but highly plausible case described by a legal commentator in the first century BC provides an illustration of the workings of the law on damages and injury. The context itself encourages insecurity: the traveller is benighted; the dark streets are the haunts of muggers. But the aggrieved owner of the torch has his rights too and he tries to enforce them through the traditional Roman methods of self-help. The thief is unknown to him and an action for theft for so small an item unviable. In the end it is the partially blinded traveller who seeks redress, through the legal remedy established by the law on criminal damage, the Lex Aquilia, a plebiscite passed in the third century in or sometime after 287 BC (R. Zimmermann 1996: 955–7). Alfenus' discussion of the case focuses not only on the remedy but also on the possible outcome and the criteria on which the court would base its decision. This would act as a guide for victims in analogous situations seeking to judge the probable outcome of their own lawsuits.

The incident, as described, also shows the workings of legal discourse in a social context. Events are driven by fear of the dark, indignation at loss of property, and the unpredictable consequences of direct action. Both parties exhibit what we would consider to be 'criminal' behaviour: the petty theft of the torch; and assault by both, leading to the serious injury of one of them. Although the consequences are not intended, the actions of both are deliberate. But Alfenus is not concerned about the morality of the theft (which is irrelevant to the action brought) or the assaults but about procedure and its likely outcomes.

DELICT AND OBLIGATION

The action brought by the half-blinded traveller was not, as observed, under 'public' procedure but the laws of delict, relating to criminal damage and injury (Watson 1970: 76–83). No definition of delict is offered by the ancient authorities, but one modern writer has defined it as 'a wrongful act, not deriving from agreement, which causes damage to another, for which the latter may recover a penalty from the wrongdoer'. Although actions were brought under civil procedures, the law of delict 'also largely served the function of criminal law, so that the redress in a private action was punitive rather than compensatory' (J. A. C. Thomas, 1975: 262; R. Zimmermann 1996: 902, 914–18).

It is in this area that we find one of the more surprising aspects of Roman legal thought on 'crime'. Under the Early Empire, if not before, such actions as theft, robbery with violence, unlawful damage and outrage are not associated in legal discourse with 'criminality' in the sense of wrong-doing but with breach of obligation. 'All obligations', wrote Gaius in the second century AD, 'are derived either from contract or from delict' (*Inst.* 3.88.182); he then proceeds to discussion of theft and actions for damages under the Lex Aquilia, to which we will return.

The treatment of certain kinds of anti-social behaviour as a form of breach of contract was to have a long history in later legal systems (R. Zimmermann 1996). Nor was legal thought the only beneficiary of the linkage; injured parties could seek redress through the less risky route of civil or praetorian process rather than embark on the hazardous route (where available) of invoking public judgements. If successful, they could expect not merely restitution but a 'penal' award of a multiple of the damages incurred or the property lost. However, for a system of penal awards to be effective, the thief or robber required the assets to pay out in the first place. When thieves were drawn from the masses of the free poor, payment of recompense was likely to be unenforceable in practice, and imperial judges therefore could impose an alternative penalty at their discretion (D. 48.19.1.3; cf. above, p. 37).

Because the law of delict could be regarded as 'serving the function' of criminal law, it was vulnerable to misunderstandings as to its character. A *delictum*, in general parlance, was a form of wrongdoing; the jurists themselves seriously compromised its technical sense when they permitted the more loaded word *maleficium* to be used as a synonym for delict (see above, p. 4). If, in popular terms, an offence such as theft was regarded as 'criminal' in the same sense as homicide, public violence or official corruption, then there was also a risk that the 'penalty' might be seen not as redress for loss but as a means of exacting 'revenge', even though revenge could not benefit the injured party in any material way. The argument of this chapter is that the perception of delict as obligation was undermined over time by social perceptions of criminality, which caused the idea of exacting a penalty through compensation to be replaced by that of revenge, which punished the wrongdoer but provided no material benefit for the victim. It will also argue that recollections of the laws of the Twelve Tables under the Empire validated the criminalisation of theft and other 'non-public' offences.

DELICT AS A CIVIL OFFENCE

The story of delict predates the formal separation of public and private and begins with certain clauses in the Twelve Tables. These clauses fixed monetary penalties for some physical injuries inflicted by one person on another (Gaius, *Inst.* 3.223); smashing a person's face with one's fist incurred 'a penalty of 300' but half that if the face was that of a slave (XII Tables 8.3); 'inflicting injury' incurred a penalty of '25' (8.4). If a limb was broken, direct and proportionate retaliation (*talio*) was permitted (8.2). These clauses established the principle that the law, now established in writing by the legislative Board of Ten, could regulate the penalties in some cases of assault, thus limiting the effects of numerous disabled Romans taking the law into their own hands. Second-century AD historians of Roman law assumed that the aim was to break the cycle of private vengeance (Gell. *NA* 20.1); however, they also conceded that the fixed penalties, being designed to apply to a relatively poor community, quickly became outdated and were replaced by awards decided by arbitration.

Juristic discourse identified a number of favourite delicts, in particular theft, *iniuria* (outrage) and unlawful damage, as first outlawed by the Lex Aquilia, to which was added robbery with violence (Gaius (*Inst.* 3.209) defined a robber as an especially wicked thief). But the Twelve Tables had also specified other forms of behaviour requiring 'penal' recompense, including the cutting down of trees belonging to other people (XII Tables 1.16/8.11) and fraud on the part of a guardian (XII Tables 8.9/20). Praetorian innovations extended the scope of delict law through the processes of actions *in factum*, or *utiles*, a flexible means of gaining redress for forms of behaviour not covered explicitly by the Edict (Watson 1974: 35, 37, 73–4). For example, the Lex Aquilia allowed only the owner of a damaged property to sue; however, the praetor's *actio utilis* allowed people with a lesser interest (such as usufruct) to seek compensation too (D. 7.1.17.3; 9.2.11.10). The praetor also added to delict law through specific civil actions. For example, the Lex Aquilia outlawed damage inflicted 'by body on body', but this was extended to cover the dropping of a precious ring in a river (D. 19.5.23). The requirement of the impact of 'body on body' could include the personal administration of a poison (D. 9.2.7.6.9.pr), or leaving poison where a slave might find it, but not actually administering it (D. 9.2.7.6). The extent of legal activity over delict shows the concern of the authorities with safeguarding the interests of citizens through due legal process rather than leaving them with scope to take the law into their own hands.

The difficulty of operating this system, for lay people, was that the laws on delict also covered behaviour which could be construed as 'criminal' by its victims. It would be hard, for example, for the layman to distinguish between unlawful killing and homicide: the jurists were careful to explain, apropos unlawful killing under the Lex Aquilia for damages, that it applied to property (and therefore slaves) not to free people (D. 9.2.2.pr. Gaius, *On the Provincial Edict*). The arrangement of the Digest suggests some confusion over what happened if the pruner of a tree killed someone by accidentally dropping a branch on his head; the jurists' opinion was that he was not liable for homicide, and Justinian's compilers underlined the point by entering Paulus' ruling both under the Lex Aquilia (D. 9.2.31) and in its chapter on the Lex Cornelia on homicide (D. 48.8.7).

THE LEX AQUILIA AND 'UNLAWFUL DAMAGE'

In or soon after 287 a *plebiscitum*, attributed to the tribune Aquilius, set out the law on unlawful or criminal damage (for details, Buckland 1966: 585–9). According to Ulpian, the Lex Aquilia superseded all previous laws on the subject (D. 9.2.1). It contained three clauses, of which the second had no long-term significance. The first chapter stated that anyone who unlawfully killed another's slave or beast classified as a *pecus*, one who feeds in herds, is liable to pay the owner the highest value achieved by the asset in the previous year (Gaius, *Inst.* 3, 210, 214; Just. *Inst.* 4.3.pr.; D. 9.2.2). The third provided a remedy for instances of unlawful damage not covered by chapter 1, by 'burning, breaking or destroying'. Those found guilty were liable for a penalty of the highest value of the asset within thirty days of the offence (Gaius, *Inst.* 3.217; Just. *Inst.* 4.3.13; D. 9.2.27.5).

Although there are numerous problems of interpretation generated by these brief texts, such as (Gaius, *On the Provincial Edict*, at D. 9.2.2.) whether elephants and camels, or bears, lions and panthers counted as parts of a *pecus* (the answers were, respectively, yes and no), and whether the thirty days ran from before or after the date of the offence, the Lex Aquilia mapped out a territory for future disputes on unlawful damage, to be assessed not by private initiatives but within the confines of the law. Early disputes reflect the priorities of a farming society. The second-century BC jurist, M. Brutus, and the pontifical author of the first 'generic' treatise on the civil law, Q. Mucius Scaevola (died 82 BC; Watson 1970: 143–58; Harries 2006a: 17–26), both addressed the question of what happened if a mare was beaten and driven out of a field belonging to another and miscarried her foal as a result. Had she been 'broken' as a consequence of being struck? The answer, in line with the generally 'commonsense' approach of commentators, was that an action could be brought if the striking or the driving had been carried out with excessive and deliberate violence (Pomponius, *On Q. Mucius* at D. 9.2.39). This broadening of the scope of 'breaking' led over time to a generalisation of the third chapter of the Lex Aquilia as referring to the 'corruption' of, or general damage to, an asset (D. 9.2.27.13).

Interpretation of the Lex Aquilia gave rise to questions of personal responsibility, negligence and accident. The jurists assumed that citizens had a duty of reasonable care when at work or play in public places. Alfenus Varus, perhaps deriving from the consular jurist Servius Sulpicius Rufus (died 43 BC), developed the implications of a plausible incident on the steep Capitoline Hill (D. 9.2.52.2). Two loaded carts are being drawn up the hill by mules and the first becomes stuck and tips up. The drivers try to lift the back of the cart to help the mules but the cart starts to roll backwards, out of control, and the drivers are forced to jump out of the way. The second cart is struck by the first and also rolls back, crushing a slave boy. The question for debate was: 'whom should the owner of the slave sue, and why?' The answer depended on the facts. Alfenus' opinion was that the drivers would be liable if they had voluntarily let go (but not if they had made the mistake of overloading the cart); the owner of the mules would be liable if the mules had shied (and therefore gone out of control). If the mules had done their best but been unable to take the weight and the cart rolled back because the drivers could not hold it, though they tried, neither drivers nor owner were liable. Later commentators might have reached different conclusions. Gaius' commentary on the Provincial Edict took the view that people were liable for the consequences of their actions if they could reasonably be anticipated. For example, if mules caused an accident because their driver failed to control them as he was not strong or experienced enough for the task, there was liability on grounds of negligence, because a man should not undertake a task if he knows that his weakness may cause danger to others (D. 9.2.8). If someone took up too heavy a load, dropped it and killed a slave, he was liable for overburdening himself in the first place; the same applied if he slipped, as he should have watched where he was going (D. 9.2.7.2). But in both of these cases the delicts would have been regarded as less serious, because (D. 9.2.32) they happened through negligence (*culpa*) not bad intent (*dolus*).

The assessment of 'culpability', therefore, depended on context. People should expect to be sued if they did dangerous things in public places, although the killing of an opponent in public wrestling and boxing matches was not unlawful, 'as the damage was inflicted in the cause of fame and courage, not by way of injury' (D. 9.2.7.4, but not applicable to slaves, who are excluded from honourable competition). Thus if people dug bear-traps and set other snares for animals in public highways and failed to put up warning notices, they could be sued if a slave or herd-animal was caught in them (D. 9.2.28 and 29); the same applied to pruners of trees, who dropped branches on public roads, without shouting a warning (9.2.31). It is characteristic of the culture of jurists that they then felt obliged to modify even these propositions and did so from relatively early in the tradition. Q. Mucius Scaevola argued that actions could also be brought for damages inflicted in private areas, as the general principle should be that negligence existed where what could be foreseen by a reasonable person had not been foreseen, or when a warning had been shouted too late for the danger to be avoided (cited by Paul, *On Sabinus*, D. 9.2.31). Paul's resolution of the issue was to insist on the presence of an access road. If there was no access, then liability would not exist, except if the defendant had deliberately thrown something at a passer-by.

Clause one of the Lex Aquilia referred to 'killing' (*occidere*), but could it also refer to 'providing the cause of death' (*causa mortis*: Nörr 1986)? While the narrow definition of 'killing' as something which was done directly 'by body on body' appears to have been maintained in juristic discourse, praetorian actions were created later to make liable those whose actions led to death, albeit indirectly. The construction of complex chains of causation, real or imaginary, allowed scope for inventiveness and ingenuity on the part not only of jurists but also of advocates in court. Is there liability if a man throws another off a bridge and he dies, whether from hitting the water, or from drowning, or from the after-effects of the fall (D.9.2.7.7)?

The jurist Celsus believed that there was, but a plausible advocate could have maintained otherwise. If someone pushed a slave off a horse and he then fell into a river and drowned, was there liability also, even though there had been no intention to push the slave into the river? A prosecuting advocate would argue from the fact of the death; the defence would argue that there had been no intention to kill. And so on.

INIURIA

The word *iniuria*, denoting unlawfulness, was open to more than one interpretation. As Ulpian carefully explained in his commentary on the Edict (D. 9.2.5.1) there were two possible meanings. One referred to something done unlawfully (for example, unlawful damage under the Lex Aquilia); the other was the offence for which the action at law on *iniuria*, outrage, could be brought (cf. Just. *Inst.* 4.4.pr.). The offence of *iniuria* referred to various kinds of insulting and offensive treatment, some, but not all, causing physical harm. The ideology of the offence is rooted in Roman beliefs in the importance of honour and reputation – which was the reason for the inability of a wife to bring a suit on behalf of her husband, as she had no honour to worry about (Just. *Inst.* 4.4.2).

There was no formal limit to the ways in which *iniuria* could be defined; in the first century AD the jurist Antistius Labeo stated that the Edict covered all cases defined as such by the action and by the courts (D. 47.10.15.26). *Iniuria* was perpetrated, for example, if a man was beaten or flogged by another and thus degraded; if he was publicly verbally abused; if his possessions were repossessed on the grounds that he was a debtor, when he was not; if he was libelled or slandered; or if his wife or young child were made the victim of stalking (Just. *Inst.* 4.4.1). As violations of honour were at the root of *iniuria*, some forms of intrusive behaviour were acceptable: it was not an offence to accost a prostitute, who could be identified by her attire, but there was room for confusion if a respectable woman was solicited by someone in the belief that she was a prostitute (D. 47.10.15.15). There were also local variations in what was acceptable and what was not; the jurists conceded that the identification of some forms of outrage depended on what the community in general held to be 'against the rules of good conduct' (*contra bonos mores* at D. 47.10.15.6).

So many and various were the forms that could be taken by outrage that the praetor's formula for the action contained a clause which allowed indication of the act on which the claim would be based. There was a further offence, aggravated outrage (*atrox iniuria*), which in Late Antiquity was assessed using a number of criteria which reflected directly on the honour of the victim. These included not only the nature of the outrage itself, but also the place where it occurred – the theatre implied an audience for the humiliation, the law courts disrespect for judges – and the status of the victim (Just. *Inst.* 4.4.9). The various manifestations of *iniuria* clearly could also involve violations of public order. Thus, although he probably did not establish a *quaestio*, the dictator Sulla did pass a law on *iniuria*, in line with his general concern with restoring peace on the streets of Rome (Ulpian at D. 47.10.5.pr.; Just. *Inst.* 4.4.8).

These violations of personal honour originated as offences against the individual, for which the praetor would provide a remedy. Evidence that feelings really had been hurt was required; a victim who 'hid' his anger was disqualified from bringing an action (D. 47.10.11.1). But, by definition, the victims of outrage were likely to be people who perceived themselves as having honour to protect and the financial resources to retaliate on their persecutors. *Iniuria*, therefore, whether or not it was made a public offence by Sulla, may have been widely accepted as such by the courts under the Empire (D. 47.10.7.6 and 37.1); certainly by the late third century the 'public' route seems to have been the one preferred (D. 47.10.45, Hermogenian). In line with the use of 'extraordinary' to denote flexibility as explained above (pp. 30–2), Justinian declared that if the public criminal litigation was successful, an 'extraordinary' penalty (*poena*) could be imposed at the discretion of the judge (Just. *Inst.* 4.4.10).

As so often, we cannot trace the process of 'criminalisation' of *iniuria*, the extent of which under the Principate is disputed (Buckland 1966: 589–92). But the legislative intervention of Sulla was significant for how seriously outrage was taken as early as the 80s BC. Vulnerable provincial governors would be obliged to respond to Roman local dignitaries who alleged 'outrage' against their fellow-citizens, with a virtually limitless charge-sheet to choose from. While, in the case of theft, the opportunities for redress may have been limited by the poverty of the offender, in cases of honour, feelings were involved and the redress sought is more likely to have been punitive than compensatory. But if this admittedly hypothetical picture is broadly correct, the 'criminalisation' of outrage was driven by the courts, not by the emperor. His was not the honour which demanded vengeance.

GELLIUS AND GAIUS ON THEFT

Although there was no 'public court' for theft, the Twelve Tables and Roman insistence on the right of self-defence created a social assumption that theft was 'criminal' in a sense that other delicts were not. It was lawful to kill the thief who came by night or burgled a house in the daytime and was found to be armed (XII Tables 1.17–18/8.12–13); it was a 'universal' legal principle that people had the right to protect their lives (cf. Cicero, *Mil.* 9). The life of the thief, therefore, was, under certain circumstances, forfeit. However, the law also established civil remedies, depending on whether the theft could be proved to be 'manifest' or not (D. 47.2.2-8). Aulus Gellius' discussion of theft and its origins provides instructive comparison with the juristic analysis of Gaius, demonstrating, as we shall see, that they drew on a shared legal and literary culture. Moreover, his 'report' of a debate between a lawyer and a philosopher on the 'cruelty' or otherwise of the provisions of the Twelve Tables (*NA* 20.1, see below, pp. 55–7) reflects conflicting standpoints on the law of theft and the desirability of the death penalty for burglars caught in the act, and it provides significant evidence of the pressures exerted by social values on the letter of the law.

But how seriously should we take Gellius on matters legal? His collection of citations of old books and discussions of things that interested him, known as the *Noctes Atticae*, the *Attic Nights*, does not instil much confidence in his ability to develop ideas in any depth. He was an amateur antiquarian and philologist, with a smattering of other disciplines. By his own account, he harboured doubts about his competence as a judge in private cases and found it especially bewildering when the evidence in a case pointed one way, and the characters of the parties the other (*NA* 14.2.4-11). When he turns to the law, he appears unable to come to terms with the world of the second century: 'neglecting the modern law, Gellius concentrates on legal history . . . his outdated notions on *furtum* indicate he rarely heard cases of this delict' (Holford-Strevens 2003: 299–300).

Is this assessment fair? Perceptions of the character of litigants and witnesses were extensively exploited by advocates, precisely because these accorded with the prejudices of judges (May 1988; Riggsby 2004). Nor was he so out of line with contemporary legal discourse as his fondness for the legal authorities of the distant past might suggest; a comparison with his near contemporary Gaius, who discussed theft as delict in his *Institutes*, and whose credentials as a legal expert are unquestioned, suggests that reference to past 'greats' such as Servius and Sabinus was common to jurists and antiquarians alike.

Gellius' interest in theft is unusually sustained and he returns to it on several occasions. The main sources for his reading of the law on theft appear to be the provisions of the Twelve Tables (which no longer applied) and one of his favourite authors, Masurius Sabinus, a younger contemporary of the emperor Tiberius, who wrote on various juristic and antiquarian themes, including a short treatise devoted to theft. Likewise, Gaius' discussion of the delict of theft opens with a list of his authorities (*Inst.* 3.183). These were Sabinus (again), Servius Sulpicius Rufus and Antistius Labeo, also from early in the first century AD. Despite this, Gaius is not usually accused of 'neglecting modern law'.

Gellius, in line with juristic interest in categories (*genera*) identifies five types of theft, which might be described as 'manifest'. First, the thief caught 'in manifest theft' could be killed if it was night or if he defended himself from arrest in the daytime with a weapon (*NA* 11.18.7). Second, the punishment for a free man taken in manifest theft was to be scourged and handed over to his victim, provided that the theft had been in daylight and no weapon had been used (11.18.8). Third, slaves taken in manifest theft were to be flogged and hurled from the Tarpeian Rock. Under-age thieves were to be flogged at the discretion of the praetor and the damage made good; this was discipline exercised by the magistrate, as boys could not be sued. Fourthly, thefts investigated through a special, and perhaps ritual, type of house-search, '*per lancem liciumque*', the meaning of which is disputed; these were punished 'as if' manifest (11.18.9). Finally, Gellius concedes that life has moved on. In his own day, an action would be brought for manifest theft for four times the value of the thing stolen (11.18.10). In this area Gaius was the more sophisticated, citing the early jurists on *genera* comparatively: Servius and Sabinus opt for four (manifest, non-manifest, *conceptum* and *oblatum*) and Labeo for two, including *conceptum* and *oblatum* as sub-categories. The comparision between authorities is an element not present in Gellius' account. However, like Gellius, Gaius includes a description of the procedures and penalties laid out in the Twelve Tables, dismissing the *lanx* and *licium* as irrelevant (*Inst.* 3.189–94).

But what was 'manifest theft'? Gellius resorted, predictably, to Sabinus' definition that manifest theft was 'one detected while being committed' and the act is completed when the stolen object reaches its destination. However, a triple penalty would be imposed in two theft-related actions at law, one against whoever received stolen goods (*furtum conceptum*) and the other brought by an innocent party who had stolen goods planted on him (*furtum oblatum*); having named these, Gellius loses interest in discussing them further (*NA* 11.18.11). 'Non-manifest theft' would incur a penalty of twice the amount stolen (11.18.15).

But Sabinus had more interesting discoveries to offer. 'Not many are aware', wrote Gellius proudly, that it was possible to 'steal' estates and houses; there had been a real case, which saw the condemnation for theft of a tenant who had sold the farm he was renting and thus 'robbed' the owner of his ownership (11.18.13). It was also possible to 'steal' people: a man had been convicted of stealing a person when he concealed a runaway slave from his master by holding out a fold of his toga, as if he was putting it on (11.18.14). For Gellius (and Sabinus) these 'decided cases' were valid sources of law.

Having reached this point, Gellius realises that he has not offered any definition of theft. Again, Sabinus comes to his rescue, offering a technical definition in the second book of his manual on civil law (11.18.19). This is based on the concept of 'unlawful touching' (*contrectatio*). Sabinus stated that 'when someone unlawfully touches the possession of another, which he should judge himself to have done against the will of the owner, he is liable to a charge of theft' (11.18.20), and that 'whoever carries off the goods of another without saying anything for the sake of gain is bound by the charge of theft, whether he knew whose it was or not' (11.18.21). Theft was also possible without the act of touching (11.18.23), therefore a master was liable if he had ordered his slave to steal something.

Although it may be conceded that the sophistication of the thinking may be that of Sabinus rather than Gellius, the anthologist's selection of topics shows his general understanding of the kinds of question that jurists (and judges) would be expected to ask. His essay covers manifest and non-manifest theft (although he does not define the latter), the penalties, past and present, for different kinds of theft, and a core definition of the offence itself, which was accepted in juristic discussion as well. He deploys Sabinus' citation of real cases and sets the offence of theft in its historical context. Nor is he dependent on Sabinus alone. In a brief excursion into comparative law, he cites the Trajanic jurist Titius Aristo (cf. Pliny, *Letters* 1.22 and 8.14) for the 'lawfulness' of theft among the Egyptians and Spartans. His juristic reading was not, therefore, entirely out of date.

Gaius' analysis of manifest theft moves beyond that of Gellius (and Sabinus). Theft is manifest if the thief is caught 'in the act' or 'in the place' (such as an olive grove or vineyard). Gaius found the extension to the thief's journey home problematic, because no time limit was agreed and 'thieves often plan to carry goods stolen in one city to other cities or provinces' (*Inst.* 3.184). He deals with the definition of non-manifest theft as 'any theft which is not manifest' and has more to say than does Gellius on *conceptum* (3.186) and *oblatum* (3.187). Like Gellius, he discusses handling (3.195–6), the thief's understanding of the expectations of the owner (3.197–8) and the extension of the definition of theft to cover unlawful uses of borrowed items, such as riding a horse on a longer journey than the one for which the animal was lent (3.196, cf. Gell. *NA* 6.15.1–2). Like Gellius, he concedes that people could be 'stolen' but ignores Gellius' (or Sabinus') case of the man with the toga. Charges of 'theft' could be brought for the kidnapping of people whose power to act independently was limited by law and dependent on another: a child-in-power; a wife under the legal control (*manus*) of her husband (not common by the second century AD); a judgement debtor or a gladiator in service (*Inst.* 3.199). Elsewhere, Gaius contradicts Gellius' reliance on Sabinus' opinion that land could be stolen (which was based on a real case); this was no longer 'accepted' opinion (*Inst.* 2.51).

Gaius' teaching manual is written with the authority of a man used to expounding the law. In line with the practice of legal interpreters, he sets his account in the context of the legal tradition but also feels free to contradict it and assert his professional authority when required. However, apart from these expressions of juristic legal culture, his account of theft is remarkably similar to that of Gellius. The same topics are covered; the same points of reference, from the fifth century BC and the first century AD, are used; some of the same controversies are aired. This is not to argue that Gellius was as good a lawyer as was Gaius; he was a reporter, rather than a questioner or an analyst of what he read. However, the comparison demonstrates a shared legal discourse on the topic of theft which stretched beyond the narrow confines of the specialist. And it shows too that the perception of theft as delict still coexisted with an older, and darker tradition. The provisions of the Twelve Tables were antiquarian and in many respects outdated. But the social assumption, that the householder had the right of self-defence against the intruder, had survived. It was therefore lawful, still, to kill out of hand the thief who came by night.

THEFT AS 'CRIME'

Did all this add up to no more than Gellius and the jurists talking to themselves? Clearly the laws of delict had practical application for every victim of theft or assault. They defined the penalties and provided actions at law through which remedies could be sought. But the emphasis on the penal nature of the awards was not adequate to counter some social perceptions that theft and assault were crimes in the fullest sense, especially when allied to the inability of the poor thief to pay even basic recompense. If financial restitution, in multiples of two or four, was not to be forthcoming anyway, then at least the victim could hope to see his wrongs 'avenged' in the criminal courts.

How out of step the specialist concern with delict and obligation could be with social mores can be illustrated through Gellius' account of the imaginary dialogue between a jurist, Sextus Caecilius, also known as Africanus, and the philosopher Favorinus of Arles at Rome in the reign of Antoninus Pius (AD 137–61). The subject of dispute was the laws of the Twelve Tables and, although part of the discussion is antiquarian, the intention of both parties was to express contemporary attitudes to the law by contrasting them with past values, a form of discourse well understood in the Second Sophistic.

Favorinus, who could criticise the laws of the Romans because his native place was Arles, complained of the Twelve Tables that they were either 'very obscure and harsh' or 'excessively mild and lax', or they were so nonsensical that they could not be interpreted as written (*NA* 20.1.4). Returning to the attack after an intervention by Sex. Caecilius, Favorinus argued that the Roman people had allowed these laws to become obsolete because they were cruel (20.1.10); that the insistence on summoning seriously ill people to court was too harsh (20.1.11); that the penalties stipulated for physical harm were derisory and had been exploited as such by a local bully, one L. Veratius, who had spent his time going round the Forum hitting people, accompanied by a slave who paid out the compensation on the spot (20.1.12–13), a scandal which had led to the replacement of the fixed penalties by awards decided by arbitration; and that the law on retaliation, as written, was unworkable because retaliation for a broken leg could not be exact and took no account of intention (20.1.14–18). The cutting up of the limbs of a debtor, to be distributed among his creditors, was also obviously inhumane (20.1.19).

This critique is no mere antiquarian set-piece. The Twelve Tables were subjects of commentary not only in the early first century by Antistius Labeo, who is cited by Favorinus for the Veratius story, but also by Gellius' contemporaries Gaius and Pomponius, both also probably based in the capital. While, naturally, seeking to parade their learning, the commentators also used the Twelve Tables as a means of analysing the law of their own time in the light of its tradition. Moreover, the criteria on which Favorinus' argument is based are social and moral, not juristic. The laws are criticised as too harsh or too lenient, or unfair; the judgement of the Roman People, who had consigned the laws to obsolescence, was all-powerful, as the 'People' were 'an assessor neither frivolous nor to be despised' (20.1.10).

Sex. Caecilius is cast as the defender of Roman law in general and the Twelve Tables in particular. He takes a historical approach and exonerates the Board of Ten, because their modern critics lack access to the 'words and ancient customs' which would allow the laws to be properly understood (20.1.6). He also appreciates the impact on law of social and political change. Like the weather or the waves of the sea, the benefits and remedies of the laws were changed and modified in line with 'the morality of the times, the systems of government, the calculation of immediate advantage and the virulence of the faults which require cure' (20.1.22). This historicist approach may be more Gellius than Caecilius but, in its dramatic context, it must also have carried conviction for Gellius' readership. The law could not be isolated from change, or from public opinion.

Equally important is that Gellius' Caecilius sees a highly rhetorical invoking of moral indignation as compatible with his juristic character:

unless you think that law is cruel which inflicts capital punishment on the judge or arbitrator lawfully appointed who is convicted of taking a bribe to influence his court decisions; or which hands over a thief caught in the act to be the slave of the man from whom he stole; or which grants the right to kill the thief who comes by night. Tell me . . . do you not think deserving of capital punishment (*capitis poena*) the treachery of a judge (*iudex*) who sells his oath for money contrary to all laws divine and human? Or the unbearable effrontery of the manifest thief caught in the act? Or the secret violence of the nocturnal bandit? (*NA* 20.1.7–8)

This is the rhetoric of the criminal law. Corrupt judges and thieves deserve punishment, because they offend against the public good. The 'capital' punishment advocated by Caecilius and backed by the authority of the Twelve Tables is not in line with the legal philosophy of delict nor is it 'compensatory' in any sense; it is about 'revenge'.

Caecilius' detailed refutation of Favorinus combines some learned etymology with his insistence that the written law must be interpreted in context. The ancient laws are defended against the charge of harshness. It was never the intention that a seriously ill person should be brought into court (*NA* 20.1.27, contrasting *morbus*, a light illness, with *morbus sonticus*, a serious disease); the transport referred to was not any old cart but a cosy covered wagon (20.1.28–30), so that the defendant could be transported in comfort but not be allowed to get away with it by malingering. As for compensation for injuries and retaliation, Favorinus had oversimplified the matter. Not all awards were trivial and the *talio* was only put into effect if the offender had refused to buy off the plaintiff (20.1.36–8). A repeated justification is that the Twelve Tables are invoked only when other means, such as arbitration or the composition of a debt, have failed.

Perhaps the most remarkable aspect of Caecilius' defence is his insistence on the importance of state terror, an attitude to be replicated by Justinian and many other Late Roman emperors. The justification was based on moral values. The debtor deserved to be treated harshly because defaulting on a debt was a breach of *fides*, faith or trust, a value dear to Romans throughout the centuries (20.1.39–40). However, there was no record of any debtor having been cut up. This, said Caecilius, was because deterrence had worked (20.1.50). Past instances of severity had also ensured future good behaviour (by others): in ancient Rome those who bore false witness were thrown from the (Tarpeian) Rock, and the faithlessness of the Alban king Mettius Fufetius, who had been torn apart by teams of horses, had been justly punished. His attitude was summed up in an elegant aphorism: 'sternness in the avenging of wrongdoing is in general the best training for living a good life, with due care' (20.1.53). These sentiments, Gellius observed, were approved by all (20.1.55).

Imaginary though this encounter may have been, the set-piece arguments of the disputants would have been consistent with modes of discourse among the Roman elite of the period on law and crime. Through antiquarian discussion of legal sanctions admitted to be obsolete, the parties asserted the importance of moral and social values for the application of the law. While Favorinus gave credit to the wisdom of the Roman People, whose humanity had rendered the harshness of the Twelve Tables obsolete, Caecilius' explanation of legal change is more complex: morality, politics, short-term self-interest, and the (perceived) prevalence of crime could all bring about legal change. But, for Caecilius, some moral values did not change. His excoriation of the corrupt judge, the burglar caught red-handed and the robber who strikes by night expresses his own views not those of the Ten, some six hundred years before, and he expects his opponent and his other auditors to share his view (as, it appears, they do). Such 'crimes' must be avenged with public severity, to deter others. In the discourse of Gellius' Caecilius no distinction is made between theft as delict and theft as 'crime', even though the emphasis on vengeance is incompatible with the legal philosophy of the penal award. Moral indignation at the wickedness of the nocturnal bandit has drowned out the principles on which the law of obligations was originally based.

CONCLUSION

The concept of the delict allowed offences against people, honour and property to be punished through the civil process, and awards of compensation with a penal element. Among legal interpreters the concept was assimilated to the law of obligations, but how far this idea achieved wider currency is uncertain. The statutory element – notably the three, or rather two, chapters of the Lex Aquilia – is very small. Delicts were dealt with through praetorian and civil-law actions and were defined by praetorian and juristic initiatives, which enabled remedies to be found for a limitless range of grievances. As they included acts of violence, theft and homicide, the conceptual difference between some delicts and public offences would have been hard to establish. Absence of redress in practice, because of the poverty of the offender or the anger of the victim, led to the imposition of other penalties, at discretion, which further eroded the distinction between private and public wrongdoing. By the third century theft could be pursued 'criminaliter', by public accusation: the device of punishment *extra ordinem* satisfied the desire of victims that 'temerity' be avenged (Ulpian at D. 47.2.93 (92)).

The 'law' of delict was therefore contested territory. In addition, the grievances for which remedies could be sought allowed scope for rhetorical, as well as juristic, interpretation. The nature of Alfenus' examples illustrates how the future jurist, as well as the advocate, was conditioned to explore issues of intention, blame and responsibility in terms both of the technical letter/spirit dichotomy and of social values in general. Once social values and consequent court decisions are allowed as influences on the development of law, the operation of legal change in the Roman world can be better understood. Laws and penalties became, in general, harsher over the period of the Empire from the first to fifth centuries AD, but this was due not only to the preoccupations of emperors but also, and perhaps more, to the prejudices of judges, and the demands of litigants not for compensation but for revenge.

CHAPTER 5

Controlling elites I: ambitus *and* repetundae

In the second century BC members of the senatorial elite initiated a process of controlling the behaviour of their peers by passing statutes which established a series of standing 'courts of investigation' (*quaestiones*). Being politicians as well as legislators, they were both the controllers and, potentially, the controlled. Their motives may have been idealistic, but they were also self-serving and practical. One problem, which they may not have perceived and certainly did not acknowledge, was that the behaviour which they hoped to control might be open to more than one interpretation. Patronage, for example, was an essential part of the operation of authority and included the exchange of gifts, not (necessarily) for purposes of enrichment but as the expression of honour and friendship. At what point did gifts become bribery, or the reception of a present extortion? When was a service to a client a form of electoral corruption (Lintott 1990)? This cultural difficulty, which affected the operation of the statutes on electoral corruption and 'extortion' or recovery (*repetundae*), illustrates the problem of legislating on offences against the public good. Too much was left to the skills of advocates, the personal influence of the defendants and the prejudices of the judges.

The standing courts were based at Rome and the *quaestio*-statutes were Rome-centred. The laws on *ambitus*, electoral corruption, referred to elections at Rome, although they could be adapted elsewhere. The Lex Lutatia *de vi* in 78 was a response to potential disturbances in the capital sparked by resistance to Sulla's confiscations (Robinson 1995: 78–80); the potential conspirator, Catiline, was threatened with prosecution under another violence-law in 63, again for disruption at Rome (Sall. *Cat.* 31.4). Statutory sanctions were also directed specifically at the powerful of the capital. A precondition for being brought before the recovery court (*repetundae*) was to have held the power to extort in the first place; electoral corruption (*ambitus*) was a candidate's crime. Provisions for the trial of governors and others accused under the *repetundae* process required the jurors to be resident in or very near Rome, and the descriptions of what was expected of them assumed a setting in the Roman Forum. Justice was socially selective, but the reach of *quaestiones* may have varied. Trials in a public *quaestio* of assassins (*sicarii*) and poisoners (*venefici*) were responses to behaviour which threatened public order (and familial solidarity). Its social reach may have been extensive (Cloud 1994: 523) but the Lex Cornelia would not have been invoked for every case of homicide in the capital: of the many murders committed in the unpoliced streets of Rome, most would have been dealt with (if they were) by magistrates through their policing powers (Nippel 1995: 5–26).

AMBITUS

Laws against electoral corruption in the Late Republic are not in themselves evidence for its extent. However, the concern of the legislators with policing the process, and their own behaviour within it, points to a perceived need for reform. Laws against corruption (see Robinson 1995: 84–6) had been passed in 181 (the Lex Cornelia Baebia) and 159 (Lex Cornelia Fulvia) but the date of the setting up of a permanent *ambitus* court is not known. Marius was tried for *ambitus* in 115 (Plut. *Mar.* 5) and the charge was frequently exploited against electoral opponents by defeated candidates (Gruen 1968a). The attraction of passing an *ambitus* law, for a politician, was that it was a demonstration of integrity; for this reason, in 67 the consul C. Calpurnius Piso and the tribune C. Cornelius competed to have their own reform passed, rather than that of their opponent (Griffin 1973). Piso's innovation may have been to extend the application of the law from the candidates to the distributors of bribes (Cic. *Mur.* 47). He also disqualified those convicted from seeking office again. Cicero's *ambitus* law of 63 in addition relegated offenders from Rome for ten years and added penalties for those who failed to turn up at their trials, pleading illness (*Planc.* 83).

The *ambitus* law could apply only when there were elections, and an electoral apparatus, to regulate (Riggsby 1999: 21). By the third century the law was a dead letter in Rome, because magistrates were appointed by the emperor (D. 48.14.1.pr.). But, as was the case with all the *quaestio*-statutes, the offence was extended and redefined. By senatorial decree, municipal magistrates were brought within its scope (D. 48.14.1.1). Then, in the late fourth century, *ambitus* acquired a new identity for the compilers of the Theodosian Code as the crime of bribing or bringing improper influence to bear on the imperial court to gain a job (*CT* 9.26.1) or to evade the rules which forbade iteration of offices (*CT* 9.26.2–4). The core definition, obtaining office by corrupt means, was still operative, but the 'electorate' was the emperor, not the *populus*.

RES REPETUNDAE

This is usually translated as 'extortion', but there are reasons why this is inappropriate when investigating the 'public' *quaestiones*. The emphasis of the procedure was on the gaining of redress for losses sustained by the prosecutor or the people he represented, not on punishing the offender as such, and was thus more in line with the 'remedial' character of Roman civil law. A more accurate equivalent of 'extortion' is *concussio*, which was recognised as a delict by imperial jurisprudence (D. 47.13.2). However, because *repetundae* under the Empire had extended to cover 'extortion', in practice the term *concussio* was applied on a lower administrative level to extortion of money by threats and intimidation. Those liable were people subject to the jurisdiction of the provincial governor, who was required to investigate allegations of perverting the course of justice by levying protection money (D. 47.13.1; 3.6.8; D. 1.18.6.3, of soldiers; *CJ* 4.7.3); also, unlawful seizure of money by tax officials was referred to their superiors (*CT* 11.7.1 = *CJ* 10.19; *CT* 9.27.7 = *CJ* 9.27.5).

Because the aim was recovery, the process of the Lex Calpurnia, which set up the first standing *quaestio* in 149 BC (Cic. *Brutus* 106), was partly based on the civil law. This was a variant of the slightly old-fashioned *legis actio sacramento* procedure (*Lex Rep.* 73–5), under which Roman citizens swore an oath before the praetor, who then appointed a *iudex*, single judge, to hear the case. Although it is possible to imagine the existence of devices within this poorly documented law which enabled non-citizens to initiate prosecutions (such as the *fictio civitatis*, which allowed litigants to pretend they were Roman citizens for purposes of the trial), it is more likely that Piso's law was a response to complaints against extortion by provincial governors, and by other magistrates including those based in Rome, brought by Roman citizens (Richardson 1987). Though still relatively few in number in the provinces, they clearly had influence, a situation which would continue after the Social War. When Cicero prosecuted Verres in 70, he insisted that he spoke for the provincials but, in fact, many of the outrages reported (mostly in the undelivered Part II) were inflicted on Roman citizens in Sicily. Piso's law modified the *legis actio* procedure by expanding the number of judges from one to perhaps 50, the number used in the Tabula Bembina (*RS* I, 65–112), a damaged text of a *Lex Repetundarum*, which is probably to be identified with C. Gracchus' law;

this generated a reshaped *legis actio* procedure, in which the accused was forced to endure the shame of a public appearance. He also stated that the damages should be assessed and made good in full but did not introduce penal restitution, at a multiple of the sum assessed.

These cosy arrangements left out the provincials. In 123–122 C. Gracchus, or a political ally, introduced a new *repetundae* law, which moved further from the civil-law prototype. The *legis actio* was replaced by another form of prosecution, the *nominis delatio*, the lodging or registration of a name, and non-citizens, including allies, Latins, foreign peoples and all within the 'discretion, jurisdiction, power and friendship of the Roman people' were allowed to bring an action; this also applied to anyone who could convince the *praetor peregrinus* that he was delegated to act by king, people or individual fellow-citizen (lines 1–4). It is not clear from this incomplete text whether or not Roman citizens could sue on their own account. In 70 Cicero stated that the *repetundae* law was for the benefit of allies, while Roman citizens could resort to civil procedures (*Div. Caec.* 17–18). It is possible that the 'civil' procedures referred to were in fact those of the Lex Calpurnia and its successor statute, the Lex Iunia, which could have continued in force alongside the new Gracchan law. Certainly, prosecutions from 122 down to the passing of the Lex Servilia Glauciae at the end of the second century were conducted exclusively by Roman citizens, but they could have been acting as *patroni* for provincial friends and clients, as allowed by the law (lines 7–12).

The Gracchan law concentrated exclusively on procedure. The praetor would establish the investigation (*praetoris quaestio esto*) and the judges (*iudices*) would conduct the trial, pass judgement and assess the award to be made. The provisions for the creation of the album of 450 *iudices* by the *praetor peregrinus*, which survive in an incomplete state, have generated most controversy. There is agreement that the courts were handed over to the '*equites*', although the clause referring to them is lost (cf. Cic. *Planc.* 32; Pliny, *Natural History* 33.32). There is no agreement as to who they were (evidence lucidly set out by Wiseman 1970). The emphasis of the text as we have it is on setting out the criteria for membership of the album in terms of the categories of people excluded. These included a number of minor magistrates (mostly non-senatorial), all past or present members of the Senate, those condemned on a public charge and therefore excluded from the Senate, those under thirty and over sixty years of age, those resident too far from Rome and people related to present or past senators, or overseas. The aim of the law was clearly to avoid the fixing of verdicts on the part of guilty magistrates and their relations or colleagues.

The same caveats applied to the selection of *iudices* from the album of 450 by the prosecutor, then the defendant. The prosecutor bound himself by a series of oaths, first that his charge was true, and secondly that he had named and thus excluded all the members of the album with whom he had any familial, friendly or professional connection. On selecting one hundred from the eligible members of the album, he had to swear publicly before the people that he had obeyed the rules of selection (lines 19–24). The defendant was then required to select fifty from the prosecutor's list without unnecessary delays (lines 24–6); the same rules on exclusions also applied.

The *praetor peregrinus* was the magistrate charged with responsibility for the proper carrying out of all the procedures. It was his job, not later than ten days after the beginning of his term of office (lines 15–18), to compose the album, in line with the exclusions specified in the statute, and publish the names in black writing on a white board; he was also obliged to read out the names to a *contio* (public meeting). He received the names of the up to forty-eight witnesses to be called and arranged for them to be summoned to testify (lines 31–5); those who had been or were still in the *fides* of either party, or their ancestors, were excluded. He oversaw the conduct of the *iudices* and enforced the penalties for misbehaviour (lines 39–46). If the accused man was convicted, the judges assessed the penalty then doubled it (lines 58–9); the praetor then ensured that the quaestor in charge of the treasury received a report and pledges guaranteeing payment (lines 56–8); if guarantees were not forthcoming, the property of the convicted man was to be seized, and the actions taken were to be placed on public record. The monies collected by the quaestor for disbursement to the victims were collected in baskets, sealed and labelled with the praetor's name, the source and the amount (lines 67–9).

The proceedings envisaged by the *Lex Repetundarum* were scrupulously recorded and public. As well as the accuser, the *iudices* were put under oath to carry out their duties properly and they were obliged to swear before the Rostra, facing towards the Forum; their names were also recited in a *contio* and written up on a board and in the public records. If there was a dispute over an individual *iudex*, the praetor was obliged to investigate publicly and, again, declare his opinion to a *contio*. If a juror failed to do his duty, by declaring more than twice that he could not reach a verdict (*non liquet*), he was liable to be heavily fined and, if he persisted, excluded from the proceedings (lines 39–46). In line with the conventions obtaining in 'public' trials, a majority of votes cast was required for conviction (lines 54–5). The voting was also public. The juror received his boxwood ballot, the dimensions of which were specified, with a black 'A' on one side (*Absolvo* = Acquit) and a black C (*Condemno*) on the other. He was to cancel one of the letters and place the ballot in the urn on the platform 'visibly according to this statute and with his arm uncovered, the letter covered by his fingers, openly' (lines 49–52); the results were then declared openly, with the ballot again shown directly to the audience. Every precaution was taken to minimise fraud and maximise the public accountability of the process.

The purpose of the law was to remove or diminish the opportunities for either party to interfere with due process and thus corrupt the verdict (see Sherwin White 1982). In itself, the text is not an anti-senatorial manifesto or a 'transfer of the court from the senate to the *equites*', although that would, of course, have been the effect. The *equites* could be defined either as the members of the eighteen equestrian centuries entitled to the public horse (*equites equo publico*) or as all male citizens with a census rating of more than 400,000 sesterces in land who were not senators. The language of exclusion favours the latter category, because the numbers of public-horse *equites* excluded would make the album unviable. Moreover, the listing of categories excluded is compatible with a vision of a jury membership which remained in the hands of the propertied classes but removed those whose association with the defendant through family relationship, patronage or business might distort the workings of justice.

The perceived efficacy of the *repetundae* laws under the Late Republic depended on views taken on the composition of the juries rather than the numbers of convictions, which themselves are no guide to the possible deterrent effect of the court's existence. Of the convictions, that of Rutilius Rufus by an equestrian jury in 92 BC was scandalous (but see Kallet-Marx 1990). In reality, as senators and *equites* alike shared the values of the propertied elite, the composition of the juries was a sideshow, but it carried symbolic importance and became a subject of political controversy (Balsdon 1938). In 106 Q. Servilius Caepio reinstated the senatorial juries. His reform was overset a few years later by the *popularis* Servilius Glaucia, who not only excluded senators, once again, but also continued Gracchus' policy of bringing the *quaestio* procedure more into line with the *iudicia populi*, permitting 'anyone who wished' (*qui volet*) to bring a prosecution. Further reform was attempted by the tribune Drusus the Younger in 91, soon after the Rutilius trial, and in 81–80 Sulla both enlarged the Senate and restored to it control of the juries in his reformed *quaestiones*. In 70 a new mixed album was created, consisting of one-third senators, one-third *equites* and one-third *tribuni aerarii*, whose identity is uncertain. In 44 the consul Antonius introduced a new panel of *iudices*, perhaps, as Cicero maintained, with the aim of packing the courts with his own supporters (*Phil.* 1.19–20; 5.12–16; 8.27; 13.3 and 37); this was repealed by Augustus (Ramsay 2005), whose Lex Julia on the public courts established their composition for the future.

Questions of the composition of the juries were a distraction from the main difficulty faced by provincials in suing Roman officials before juries of other wealthy Roman citizens, which was to persuade their audience of their sincerity. A skilled defence advocate – a Cicero, for example – could undermine provincial accusers by playing on the stereotypes of the foreigner, the primitive and bellicose accusers of Fonteius, former governor of Transalpine Gaul in 69 (*Font.* 27–36), or the shifty Greeks who attacked the virtuous Flaccus in the 50s. With these would be contrasted the allegedly upright, Roman character of the accused and his previous public services. These techniques of persuasion were reinforced by the collective self-interest of rich Romans. Neither senatorial governors nor equestrian *publicani* and businessmen had any interest in safeguarding the general welfare of provincials, apart from their own clients; their indifference was reinforced by their relationships in politics and business with each other. Even Cicero, who tried very hard as governor of Cilicia to limit abuses in 51–50, avoided direct confrontation with his political ally M. Brutus, whom he knew to be violently oppressing, through his agent, the town councillors of Salamis in Cyprus (*Att.* 5.21; 6.1–2).

REPETUNDAE UNDER THE EMPIRE

The Julian Law on *repetundae* was the governing statute for recovery proceedings under the Empire. The law and its later commentators established that certain forms of behaviour created liability; statutory provision had therefore moved beyond the Gracchan thinking to encompass definitions of actions for which remedies could be sought under the law. Governors of provinces were, of course, liable, but so too were their staffs and advisors, and any magistrate, administrator or holder of a position of power. The receipt of bribes to pervert the course of justice was especially frowned upon: governors and other officials were forbidden to receive money concerning any judicial act, including accusations, the giving or withholding of evidence and the delivery of the verdict (D. 48.11.3; 6; 7). Delegation of judicial responsibility in criminal cases was not permitted; in civil cases, the governor could not be influenced by money in his choice of a judge (D. 48.11.7). The Lex Julia was also explicit that presents above a

certain value were not permitted, except from close relations and wives
(D. 48.11.1.1).

Repetundae was a *publicum iudicium* (cf. D. 48.1.1) and therefore part of
the *ordo*, as the imperial jurists saw it, of offences categorised as public.
However, its original formulation, as we have seen, contained elements
from the law of delict, where the penalty was compensation with a penal
element. Its assimilation to other public offences under the Empire created
an expectation that the penalty would be assimilated to those inflicted as
the *poena legis*, or punishment specified in the text of other public criminal
statutes. Thus, like the others, the purpose of the *repetundae* law would
come to be viewed as retribution as well as (or instead of) restitution.
Consequently, offenders came to incur punishment *extra ordinem*, not
because the offence was 'extra-ordinary' but because the punishment was
not the type originally envisaged by the statute. 'Today', wrote Aemilius
Macer, 'they are punished under the Lex Repetundarum *extra ordinem*, and
mostly are punished with exile and even harsher sentences, in proportion to
the seriousness of their offence' (D. 48.11.7.3). Capital punishment could
be inflicted on those governors who connived at the execution of innocent
men for money, or even on those who caused the death of an innocent man
out of rage; they could expect perhaps death, and certainly deportation to
an island.

But what were the chances of conviction and appropriate sentencing in
practice? Under the Republic relatively few corrupt governors had received
their deserts, because the self-interest of the wealthy and Roman parochi-
alism prevailed over the requirements of justice. Under the Empire the
quaestio de repetundis at Rome seems to have been quickly superseded by
the Senate, which took over the task of judging its own members. The
presence of a hardworking emperor at these sessions helped to curtail some
abuses though not all (Brunt 1961). This and the expansion of the Roman
citizenship in the provinces gave the provincials more of a voice in the
capital. But two *repetundae* trials recorded by Pliny the Younger show
senatorial solidarity still at work to limit the consequences of malpractice.

In AD 100 the corrupt governor of Africa, Marius Priscus, pleaded guilty
to the charge of *repetundae* before the Senate and demanded a board of
assessors (*recuperatores*) to decide on the award to the provincials (Pliny,
Letters 2.11 and 12; see also Robinson 2006: ch. 4). However, the prosecutors, Pliny the Younger and Cornelius Tacitus, the latter better known
then as an orator than as a historian, vigorously opposed this because
Priscus had also condemned and executed innocent people. A dispute
broke out as to whether the Senate was empowered to hear a case where

the accused had already pleaded guilty; advocates of stern measures insisted that the punishment should fit the crime. In the end the Senate (as usual) compromised and agreed that assessors should be appointed, and that they would also hear about the accusations of judicial corruption.

The trial illustrates why the law encompassed the behaviour of officials, as well as that of the governors themselves. Two of Priscus' associates had, allegedly, bribed judges to pass capital sentences (an offence under the Lex Cornelia on homicide, which included perverting the course of justice in serious cases). One had given 300,000 sesterces for the conviction and exile of a Roman *eques* and the conviction on capital charges of seven of his friends. This character had conveniently died. The second, one Flavius Marcianus, had given 700,000 sesterces to have another Roman *eques* beaten, sent to the mines and strangled in prison, treatment that was inappropriate for any Roman citizen. Marcianus was brought to trial before the Senate, where he implicated Priscus' legate, Hostilius Vitellius, as one who had received a large bribe and fiddled the accounts to award himself 10,000HS in 'ointment-money'. As Vitellius was absent, the Senate agreed to deal with him later.

Speeches were made for and against Marcianus and Priscus over a period of three days; Pliny was on his feet for five hours, although he worried (so he said) that feelings of 'compassion' on the part of his colleagues might make his task harder. At the end of this prolonged session there were two proposals as to sentence. The first was that Priscus repay 700,000 sesterces and be banished from Italy, while Marcianus should be banished from Africa too; the second confined Priscus' punishment to the payment of the fine (or restitution) and limited Marcianus' banishment to five years. The former proposal was adopted. However, when it came to the trial of Vitellius, the Senate, again, found itself required to choose between two penalties: expulsion from the Senate, or exclusion from being considered for future provincial governorships in the Senate's control. The Senate chose the latter, more lenient option, to Pliny's disgust.

The Senate could thus congratulate itself on justice done, unlike the oppressed province of Africa, which, according to Juvenal, failed to benefit at all from the 'recovery' process (*Sat.* 1.50). But Pliny's worries about the effects of compassion on the operation of justice were well founded, not least because he was subject to them himself. When defending the former governor of Bithynia, Julius Bassus, two years later, Pliny commented on the pity that all must feel for this man with his unlucky record of prosecutions and his regrettable misunderstanding of the Lex Julia *repetundarum*, which explicitly forbade the acceptance of gifts from provincials (*Letter* 4.9). Pliny's intention as defence advocate was to employ a cautious

combination of several lines of argument, including vilification of the
Bithynian delegate, a verbose, tactless and possibly criminal character,
but he found it impossible to deny that the law had been broken. Bassus
was duly found guilty but the Senate then exercised its right to mitigate the
punishment of this poor old man, out of compassion, and because the
taking of presents, although illegal, was 'not uncommon'.

These two vignettes of the operation of senatorial justice do not encourage confidence in the ability of the senators to be severe with their own.
Group solidarity and some xenophobia appear still to operate, as they did
under the Late Republic. However, there had been some changes for the
better. At the trial of Marcianus and Priscus, the emperor himself presided;
senators could not therefore move too obviously out of line and could not
be seen to exonerate the guilty. Moreover, the provincial presence itself was
more assertive. This could have effects of another kind. Not all accusations
of provincial maladministration were true. Pliny had doubts as to the good
faith of Theophanes, one of Bassus' prosecutors, which appear to have been
shared by other senators. Provincial rivalries and grudges could inspire
ungrounded accusations of corrupt behaviour. When another Bithynian
governor, Varenus Rufus, was also accused, shortly after the Bassus trial
(Pliny, *Letter* 5.20), the Senate found itself confronted by two delegations
from Bithynia, one in favour of Varenus and the other against, and both
claiming to represent the provincial council (*Letters* 6.5, 6.13, 7.6). Not
surprisingly, Pliny, in Bithynia as a special legate from *c.* 110, made a point
of referring every controversial decision to the emperor, partly in order to
head off invidious accusations on his return.

REPETUNDAE IN LATE ANTIQUITY

Late in the third century Diocletian (AD 284–305) reformed the provincial
structure of the entire Roman Empire, creating a number of small provinces (Jones 1964: 42–6). The governors of these had mainly judicial
functions and were thus often called simply *iudices*, judges. Two further
layers of provincial official were placed above them: the praetorian prefect
and his deputies, or *vicarii*. The governors were the courts of first resort but
litigants had extensive rights of appeal – and they were all now citizens.
Moreover, the rhetoric of some imperial legislation even encouraged
accusers to come forward if they had been the victim of extortion: if they
reported and could prove their accusation, they could gain 'great honour
and reputation' (*CT* 9.27.6) thereby – although recovery of lost assets is not
stipulated in the extant text.

Contrary to Macer's pronouncement that conviction for *repetundae* entailed exile or worse, the corrupt governor and his officials in Late Antiquity could expect to get off with a fine. This was a rare example of comparative leniency in Late Antique judicial practice but was also in line with the general official culture of the period, which reverted to earlier practice in stipulating fines as penalties for official misconduct. However, fines are not levied on the same principles as assessments for recovery or restitution, which could still be found in operation. In 382 one Natalis was condemned to be returned under imperial guard to the province he and his officials had plundered and to repay the money extorted fourfold (*CT* 9.27.3), although it is not clear how far the provincials themselves would benefit.

A word on fines as penalties for official misconduct is in order. Fines were the means by which the community or the state compensated itself for the failures of its agents. The principle obtained in the Republic. The *Lex Repetundarum* specified that jurors who misbehaved would incur the 'supreme fine' (lines 45–6). However, the fine as penalty really came into its own in the context of the bureaucratic culture of the fourth and fifth centuries AD. The sum to be paid was determined by weight of precious metals, not by coinage, thus avoiding devaluation of the fine due to the debasement of the coinage. The aim was to enforce obedience to imperial regulations on the part of officials by penalising those who failed to observe or implement them; fines tended to be higher in the Eastern Empire than they were in the West, because the East was wealthier (Honoré 1998: 26–9).

Fines were also part of the rhetoric of legislation aimed at controlling official abuse. Valentinian I, who was a Christian, warned the Elder Symmachus, Prefect of Rome, that Christians were not to be condemned to the arena and that a judge who did so would be 'severely censured' and his office staff punished 'with a very heavy fine' (*CT* 9.40.8, of 365). On other occasions emperors became more specific. Warned that convicts were being rescued from the courts by assertive Christian clerics and fraudulent appeals, Theodosius I instructed his praetorian prefect that, if this was to continue to happen, governors would suffer the stigma of *infamia* and that the upper ranks would be fined thirty pounds of gold, the lower ranks fifteen. The law emphasised the responsibilities of the office staffs, who would be fined if they had failed to advise the governor about the law; they were also expected to intervene personally to prevent the removal of the convicted people and ensure that the sentence was carried out (*CT* 9.40.15, of 392). However, further reflection suggested that Christian direct action might be hard for officials to control in practice and it was conceded that reference to the emperor could be made if the local authorities feared 'a war, rather than a legal hearing' (*CT* 9.40.16, of 398).

The liabilities of office staffs were now more strictly defined than they had been in Pliny's day, when there was no surprise if a corrupt governor infected his associates. The Late Roman official was expected to know the regulations, even if his governor did not, and to ensure that they were enforced. If the office staff of the Prefect of the Corn Supply at Rome did not intervene to prevent members of the bakers' guild from escaping their duties by marrying outside it, they were fined ten pounds of gold (*CT* 14.4.21). If a governor overruled an imperial judgement, his staff would be fined five pounds of gold for failing to inform him of the law, and he would pay ten (*CT* 1.6.9). Governors who failed to enforce Theodosius I's prohibition of pagan sacrifices and rituals (or who indulged in them themselves) were fined fifteen pounds of gold for personal violation and thirty for failure to enforce the law; the same applied to the staffs (*CT* 16.1.0.11, of 391 and 12, of 392). Fines were also levied for failure to follow legal procedures within specified time limits; documents relating to appeals were to be forwarded within thirty days of the original hearing, and failure to do so would result in *infamia* and a fine of ten pounds of gold, while the administrators would be liable for double the amount (*CT* 11.30.34, of 364). Even unlawful delegation of powers to a legate now incurred a heavy sanction: thirty pounds of gold would be extracted from both governor and his delegate, and from the office staffs as well, if they had failed to protest (*CT* 1.12.8, of 400).

CONCLUSION: ELITE SELF-REGULATION AND ITS LIMITS

The *repetundae* laws were created under the Republic for a specific and limited purpose, to enable actions for the recovery of assets extorted from the provincials. A succession of laws on the matter were proposed and passed by senators, who believed that abuses of provincial government by fellow-members of their order should be checked, and the victims recompensed. The process enabled the full participation of the provincials, although in practice they preferred to resort to Roman *patroni*. The early statutes appear to have offered no definition of what forms of extortion or malpractice were covered by the *quaestio*; this omission was rectified in the later statutes and, under the Empire, in juristic commentaries.

The original *repetundae* statutes shared some of the characteristics of the laws of delict. They concerned wrongdoing, which entailed a financial penalty, assessed on the basis of restitution of the original asset, plus the multiple, the penal element. The reason for resort to delictal procedure in general was that the victim hoped to recover his losses and more. The aim, therefore, was not retribution or 'revenge'. However, the later assimilation of *repetundae* statutes to other *publica iudicia*, where retribution was a more obvious motive, changed the character of the offence, a development encouraged by the inclusion of other forms of misconduct on the part of governors. After a phase in which outright punishment was preferred, if Macer is to be believed, the compensatory nature of the 'recovery process' and its penalty appears to have reasserted itself, a development assisted by the Late Roman culture of official accountability both to the subjects of the Empire, who were encouraged to inform on bad governors, and to the supposedly all-seeing emperor.

But why did the elite resort to self-regulation in the first place? While genuine concern for good government cannot be ruled out, virtuous legislation not only enhanced prestige but also favoured the legislator in the fierce senatorial competition for votes, office and influence. The legislative programme of C. Gracchus as a whole was designed to further senatorial accountability to the *populus*. This would have enhanced his standing, and his chances in future elections, where he could hope to rely on a coalition of appreciative clients and grateful *equites*. Also, appearances mattered, even if the reality was very different. Governors could not be seen to be bad and getting away with it. Verres, when prosecuted by Cicero for the Sicilians in 70, was forced to anticipate sentence by exile; the weight of testimony collected by his energetic prosecutor outweighed the powerful coalition of friends and relations in high places, on whom he had relied to secure his acquittal.

Republican politicians and governors were self-policing, answerable to their colleagues but not subject to them. When an allegedly corrupt governor was brought to trial, the tendency to acquit suggests that the collective self-interest of the propertied elite outweighed competitive considerations. Under the Empire the balance shifted gradually but decisively in favour of the emperor and the aggrieved provincials. Governors could be summoned to account, even when the Senate might be slow to redress their full grievance because of 'pity' for their colleague. As the power of the Senate itself diminished, so the direct control of the emperor over his governors increased. The rhetoric of imperial legislation, especially that of Late Antiquity, which survives through extracts in the Codes, stresses the accountability of officials and of governors. The new-style *repetundae* and *ambitus* were shaped by the agenda of the supreme controller of rulers and ruled alike.

CHAPTER 6

Controlling elites II: maiestas

Treason was the worst of crimes. *Perduellio,* or 'acting like an enemy (*perduellis*)' menaced the safety of the whole community, and its punishment was correspondingly harsh: the traitor would be publicly flogged and crucified. The Twelve Tables ordained punishment for 'the man who incites an enemy or who hands over a citizen to an enemy' (D. 48.4.3). Tacitus' brief sketch of the treason law at the start of Tiberius' reign merged *perduellio* with 'damage to' *maiestas* (for their use in accusations, see Rogers 1933) and reminded his readers that the law encompassed the betrayal of an army, seditious incitement of the people and any act by which 'the *maiestas* of the Roman people was diminished' (*Ann.* 1.72). Problems of definition and the strong feelings aroused by alleged abuse of the charge for private gain can obscure the importance and seriousness of the offence.

FROM SATURNINUS TO CAESAR

The merging of the ancient crime of treason and the offence of *maiestas* was probably due to a law of L. Appuleius Saturninus in 103 or 100 BC (despite attestation of earlier use of the term). The original context of Saturninus' reform was political and highly partisan. Saturninus' reforms in general extended the power of the *populus* over its executive, the magistrates and Senate, and included active interference in the administration of the provinces and provincial commands (as in the Delphic Piracy Law) and the imposition of oaths on senators that they would obey the laws (Lintott 1994: 95–101). In line with this, the *maiestas* law was born out of a desire to control the behaviour of the military and political elite by making them legally accountable for damage to the 'greatness' of the Roman People (Ferrary 1983).

Recent history strengthened his hand. By the late second century BC the Roman People had become impatient with the perceived incompetence of their generals; failure was treasonable, whether intended or not. C. Plautius, praetor in Spain in 146, lost four legions in battle and himself escaped by running away; he was indicted for *perduellio* as a result (App. *Iberica* 64; Livy, *Per.* 52). In a spate of tribunician prosecutions in the last decade of the second century generals and their legates were held to account for surrendering (but also saving) their armies (C. Popilius Laenas, 106 BC, in Cic. *Inv.* 2.72–3; *Leg.* 3.36; *Rhet. ad Her.* 1.25; 4.34; Oros. 5.15.24); and for attacking the Cimbri without authorisation from the people (M. Junius Silanus, who was acquitted, Asc. *Corn.* 80, Lewis 2006: 288; Cic. *Div. Caec.* 67).

Their problems were exacerbated by the political hysteria generated by the perceived failure of the Senate to deal efficiently with Jugurtha. 'To a most bitter enemy', said Sallust's Memmius, 'the authority of the Senate has been betrayed, your Empire has been betrayed; at home and on the field of battle the *res publica* has been put up for sale' (Sall. *Jug.* 31). Those guilty of both unintentional but still culpable failure and deliberate collusion found their nemesis in the *quaestio Mamilia*, a special court set up in 109 (Cic. *Brutus* 128; Sall. *Jug.* 40). This condemned for treason and exiled those responsible for failures in Africa; the court also condemned L. Opimius, the consul responsible for the deaths of C. Gracchus and his supporters in 121. In the same period the use of the secret ballot was extended to capital cases, including *perduellio*, heard by the people. In 103, in the aftermath of the catastrophic Roman defeat at Arausio, Saturninus and his associate Norbanus prosecuted for *perduellio* both the consulars responsible, Q. Servilius Caepio (consul in 106), a noted champion of senatorial privilege, and C. Mallius Maximus (*Auct. ad Her.* 1.24; Livy, *Per.* 67). Both were exiled.

Saturninus' *maiestas* law reflected the assumption present in the *perduellio* trials of the previous few years, that treason was a crime against the people. The *maiestas* law did not replace *perduellio*; soon after its passing Metellus Numidicus was prosecuted for *perduellio* for failing to swear to uphold a measure on the distribution of land in Gaul (cf. Cic. *Clu.* 95; Appian, *Civil Wars* 1.4.29–31) and 'interdicted from fire and water' (Gruen 1965). However, the new law supplemented it by introducing a new (and characteristic) emphasis on the sovereign 'greatness' of the people. Those who 'diminished' or 'damaged' the *maiestas* of the people could expect retribution. Yet, paradoxically, the probable setting up of a standing court (*publica quaestio*, Val. Max. 8.5.2; Cloud 1994: 518–20) diminished the role of the *populus* as judge in its own case through the assemblies.

A fragmentary inscription from Tarentum has been identified by some with the Lex Appuleia (e.g. Bauman 1967: 50–5). It insists that the statute be supported on oath, on pain of sanctions for those who refuse, a provision which reflected Saturninus' consistent emphasis on popular accountability on the part of the Senate. However, another clause in the Tarentine fragment, which offers rewards for non-citizen prosecutors, appears incompatible with the principle that injuries to the *maiestas* of the Roman people should be the unique concern of Roman citizens (*RS* I, 209–19); ascription to a *Lex Repetundarum* is therefore preferred (where the power to prosecute by non-citizens is well attested). That said, Saturninus may simply have been inconsistent; too much should not be expected of the logical processes of some Roman politicians.

It is not known if the Lex Appuleia offered a definition of what kinds of activities would damage or diminish the *maiestas* of the *populus*. In line with its popular character, Saturninus may have left it to the *populus* to decide. The definition offered by Cicero, writing in the early 80s, was derogation from the *maiestas*, *dignitas* (honour) and *amplitudo* (greatness, again) of the Roman People and those to whom the Roman People had granted power (*Inv.* 2.17); the law may have said no more. The result of inadequate definition, or none at all, was a wealth of opportunities offered to advocates.

For the author of the *Rhetorica ad Herennium*, of the 80s BC, arguments about *maiestas* hinged on *definitio*. To illustrate such a case, he recorded a set of manoeuvres which resulted in the indictment in 95 of Q. Servilius Caepio the younger (son of the consul of 106) for *maiestas* (*Rhet. ad Her.* 1.12.21). Caepio, as quaestor in 103, had advised the Senate that Saturninus' grain law was too expensive and the Senate, in line with his advice, decreed that it was against the public interest to take the bill to the People. Saturninus did so regardless and was vetoed by his colleagues. When Saturninus persisted, Caepio resorted to direct action and attacked the meeting, throwing down the voting bridges. Eight years later (and four after Saturninus' death) Caepio was indicted. 'This', commented the Rhetor, 'is the legal issue concerning definition, for the word is itself defined when the investigation concerns what it is "to diminish greatness".' The advocates on both sides would therefore offer their conflicting definitions of *maiestas*, on the lines of 'he diminishes *maiestas* who . . .'. The prosecution asserts that 'he damages *maiestas*, who destroys the constituent parts of the "greatness" of the *civitas* or citizen body', by which was meant the votes of the *populus* and the council of the magistrates. Caepio's defence would run that *maiestas* meant to cause real damage to the greatness of the *civitas* and that he had in fact prevented such damage by protecting the treasury and refusing to acquiesce in the destruction of the *maiestas* of the people.

Cicero would later (*De or.* 2.107–9) insist that the good advocate should not appear to offer a definition when doing so. In another trial of the mid-90s (Cic. *De or.* 2.107–9; Val. Max. 8.5.2; Badian 1957), M. Antonius appeared for Saturninus' ally Norbanus, who had admitted to violence against prominent public figures, including the stoning of the eminent M. Aemilius Scaurus, and a riot in a temple. Antonius developed the concept of the justified riot, as Norbanus was acting in the people's interest against the unpopular Caepio. Secondly, he emphasised the ties of personal duty, *pietas*, which bound him to his former quaestor. He did not spell out the negative definition implicit in his argument; violence in the interests of the *populus* could not reasonably be construed as diminishing their *maiestas*. The judges agreed and acquitted Norbanus.

Although court decisions did not provide formal or binding precedents, the arguments of advocates were crucial for shaping the discourse on public offences. Arguments and previous court decisions could be adduced by advocates in support of their general argument, to add to its 'persuasiveness'; if the decisions were conflicting, the advocate could assess 'the judges, the context and the number of decisions' (*Rhet. ad Her.* 2.46). Moreover, advocates could resort to argument from ambiguity. In 50 Cicero complained to Appius Claudius that even after Sulla's attempts to clarify matters, *maiestas* was still *ambigua* (*Fam.* 3.11.2). Ambiguity was another gift to the advocate, who could resort to arguments extraneous to the text, such as whether an argument or decision was consistent with what was 'honorable, upright, statutory, customary, natural or in line with the good and the fair' (*Rhet. ad Her.* 2.11.16).

In the late 80s the dictator Sulla attempted a clarification of the *maiestas* law to inhibit frivolous prosecutions (Cic. *Fam.* 3.11.2) but failed to solve the basic difficulty of defining the offence itself (Cloud 1994: 520). However, his work was effective in ensuring the permanent replacement of *perduellio* with *maiestas*, which now became 'treason' in every sense. To the two previous broad categories – criminal incompetence and deliberate collusion with an enemy – was now added any form of behaviour on the part of holders of *imperium*, and perhaps other magistrates and officials as well, which was unauthorised by Senate and People. Provincial governors were forbidden to leave their province or to lead an army across provincial boundaries, nor could they venture into client-kingdoms without authorisation (Cic. *Pis.* 50). The strengthening of the accountability of magistrates to the People, which had driven the *popularis* Saturninus, was systematised in the legislation of his political opposite, the champion of the existing order.

Both the military and the political dimensions of the *maiestas* law were tested in the decades which followed. One Bulbus was charged with tampering with a legion in Illyricum (Cic. *Clu.* 97); and a certain Staienus allegedly fomented sedition in the army when serving as quaestor (*Clu.* 99). A political defendant, C. Cornelius, tribune in 67, was accused of *maiestas* in 65 on the grounds that he had overridden a tribunician veto, read out his bill himself when his *scriba* was prevented from doing so by his fellow-tribune, and ignored the protests of the then consul, C. Calpurnius Piso (Griffin 1973). Cornelius was lucky in that the relative moderation of his own conduct and the skills of his advocate, the ex-praetor Cicero, combined to acquit him. Cicero's argument was a variant of Antonius' for Norbanus, that Cornelius' actions were in the public interest and had precedent in those of his colleague Gabinius (Asc. *Corn.* 71-2C, Lewis 2006: 278). The 'ambiguity' of *maiestas* favoured the politicising of the offence and the issuing of verdicts based on criteria other than the merits of the case. In the late 50s Appius Claudius Pulcher was prosecuted for *maiestas*, rather than embezzlement, and was defended or assisted by Pompey, young Brutus and 'the whole *res publica*'. Cicero's comment (*Fam.* 3.11) on the outcome was that, of course, Appius would have been acquitted on either charge, but in the case of embezzlement there was a clear divide between guilt and innocence (i.e. that the outcome would have been harder to fix).

The legacy of the Republic to the Empire in defining treason was itself ambiguous (Levick 1976: 183–4; Rutledge 2001: 87–9). Treason was the worst of crimes, and the most political. A string of trials had shown its usefulness for the pursuit of senatorial rivalries through the public criminal courts, adding a dangerous new dimension to political competition. When Sulla and, later, Caesar's Lex Julia *maiestatis* (Allison and Cloud 1962) attempted to curb the abuse of the statute, their success was limited. Neither Sulla nor Caesar, whose *lex maiestatis* is referred to by Cicero in 44 (*Phil.* 1.9.23), had much credibility as legislators who forbade governors to leave their provinces without permission, when both had notoriously done so to further their own careers.

Sulla perhaps and Caesar certainly made an effort to list the offences which fell under the law. The Lex Julia *maiestatis* was the master-statute for the Empire and its jurists. Ulpian's account in the third century (D. 48.4.1) may be true to its contents in outline (including specific references to Rome), although there were also anachronistic references to imperial fiats, probably added later:

The charge (*crimen*) of *maiestas* refers to an action which is committed against the *populus Romanus* or its safety. He is liable by whose agency with deliberate malicious intent a plot is entered into to kill hostages [without the order of the emperor]; or that men should be within or assemble within the bounds of the city armed with weapons or stones against the interests of the *res publica*, or that they should seize control of sites or temples, or that there should be a ganging-up or assembly, or that men should be brought together for seditious ends; or by whose agency and deliberate bad intent a conspiracy should be entered into to kill any magistrate of the Roman People, or anyone holding *imperium*, or other form of official power (*potestas*); or that anyone should bear arms against the *res publica*; or that anyone should send a messenger or letters to an enemy of the Roman People, or give them a password or should so act with deliberate bad intent that enemies of the Roman People receive assistance from his advice against the *res publica*; or who persuades or incites soldiers in such a way as to give rise to sedition or revolts against the *res publica*.

Ulpian's excerpting of the Lex Julia reveals that Caesar, and perhaps Sulla before him, concentrated on *perduellio*, the security, rather than the *maiestas*, of the Roman People, allowing for the parallel development of both elements within the same law. The statute focused on public order in Rome, with the banning of organisation of violent sedition and the seizure of important buildings, and of plots to murder Roman magistrates. A second dimension is the traditionally military: correspondence or collusion with the enemy was treason, as also was desertion and the incitement of disorder in the ranks. And thirdly, the laws tried to control the generals who headed armies as governors in the provinces. Both Ulpian and Marcian reveal the dependence of the Lex Julia on Sulla's law with regard to the behaviour of provincial governors. The Julian law of *maiestas* applied to governors who failed to leave their province after their successor had arrived (Marcian at D. 48.4.2); the time allowed for the overlap by the Lex Cornelia was no more than thirty days (Cic. *Fam.* 3.6.3).

MAIESTAS UNDER THE EMPIRE

No new legislation was enacted on treason under the Empire, although the possibility of a law re-enacting that of Caesar by Augustus cannot be entirely discounted. Instead, the offence and its punishment evolved through a series of cases, often though not always heard by the Senate, and decided by imperial fiat. The most notorious aspect of its evolution in the Early Principate was the assimilation of the *maiestas* of the People to that of the emperor, thus bringing damage to his greatness within the compass of the law. This was helped by the original terms of Saturninus' law, that it applied to those who derogated from the greatness of magistrates, as well as of the People.

The *quaestio de maiestate* continued in operation in the early years of Augustus. Marcus Primus was tried before it for waging war outside Macedonia without authorisation and convicted by a narrow margin (Dio 54.3.2–3). Soon afterwards Fannius Caepio and Varro Murena were prosecuted before a panel of judges and convicted *in absentia*, to be executed later (Suet. *Tib.* 8.1; Dio 54.3.4–8). The infliction of the death penalty on Caepio and Murena signalled another important development. The *poena legis*, the penalty established by the *maiestas* law, was interdiction from fire and water (but see Levick 1979). This was true after Caesar's law (Cic. *Phil.* 1.9.23) and was still the case in the reign of Tiberius (*SC de Pisone patre* 120–3). However, emperors as magistrates believed they could exercise discretion over the penalties imposed. Late in life Augustus hoped to inflict a harsher punishment on his granddaughter's lover, D. Junius Silanus, because his seduction of Julia the younger had been an offence against religion and a 'violation' of *maiestas* as well (Tac. *Ann.* 3.24, cf. Suet. *Claud.* 14 for Claudius' sentencing of fraudsters to the arena, a harsher penalty than the law allowed). Under Tiberius, however, and supported by the Caepio and Murena precedent, the senatorial judges of *maiestas* and other cases resorted to the death penalty, often regardless of the severity of the offence. And Pliny's accounts of the trials for *repetundae* of Marius Priscus' associates in Africa and of Julius Bassus (*Letter* 4.9.17) are evidence for the Senate's continuing power to mitigate or strengthen the penalties of the law.

From the limited evidence Augustus appears to have been reluctant to resort to the public *maiestas* procedure. It is not clear from the sources how the alleged lovers of Julia the elder were disposed of in 2 BC (Vell. Pat. 2.100.4–5; Tac. *Ann.* 1.70.3; 3.18.2; 4.44.5; Dio 55.10). One significant development was the apparent extension of the *maiestas* accusation to cover dangerously defamatory writings (Tac. *Ann.* 1.72.3–4; Dio 55.4.3, on Cassius Severus), which was further developed under Tiberius in the prosecution of Cremutius Cordus, who had published his work, the *Annales*, under Augustus without incurring censure (Tac. *Ann.* 4.34–6; Suet. *Aug.* 35; Dio 57.24.2–4).

Despite this, the *quaestio de maiestate* appears to have fallen into abeyance in the latter years of Augustus and, soon after his accession, Tiberius was asked by the praetor Pompeius Macer if he wished for the restoration of the *iudicia*. Tiberius replied that the law should be enforced (Tac. *Ann.* 1.72–3). Had this been done, the praetor would have presided. Instead, the first cases were heard under the presidency of the consuls (who were told to acquit two men charged with minor disrespect to Augustus) and then before the Senate itself. Although, as the *SC de Pisone patre* reveals (vv. 120–3; Richardson 1997), the form of the judgement was a recommendation to the praetor in charge of the court, in practice the ancient *quaestio* was now sidelined.

Senatorial decrees as legal judgements or recommendations became part of the legal baggage carried by the *maiestas* charge. In that sense, *maiestas* was in part the creation of case law. According to tradition, the Roman People had endorsed Horatius' killing of his sister for mourning the death of her lover, who was serving with the enemy (Livy 1.26). That provided a historical precedent for three decrees from the 20s and 30s which forbade mourning for those convicted of treason, including Piso and Sejanus (Dio 58.12.4; 16.6); this even extended to a mother, denied the right to mourn her 'traitor' son (Tac. *Ann.* 6.10). This principle was repeated in juristic writing: Ulpian stated that mourning was not permitted for public enemies, those convicted of treason and those who killed themselves out of guilt (D. 3.2.11.3). A second senatorial decree, with reference to the delict of outrage (*iniuria*), imprisoned one Annia Rufilla, who had taken refuge with an imperial image (Tac. *Ann.* 3.36); the jurist Cervidius Scaevola referred to a *senatusconsultum* which threatened with imprisonment anyone who exploited the image of the emperor to the detriment of another (D. 47.10.38).

Imperial statues were always problematic. To what extent did they represent the emperor, and under what circumstances? The first test case of Tiberius' reign concerned the *eques* Falanius, who had *inter alia* included a statue of Augustus in the sale of his gardens (Tac. *Ann.* 1.73) – and who was acquitted on the emperor's order. A second-century jurist stated that those who melted down statues of emperors which had been consecrated were liable for *maiestas* (D. 48.4.6) but those who melted down rejected statues were not liable, nor was a man who had restored imperial statues which had fallen into disrepair. Septimius and Caracalla ruled that anyone who accidentally hit a statue of an emperor with a stone was not liable, nor were those who sold likenesses of emperors which had not yet been consecrated (D. 48.4.5).

Maiestas was both uncertain and deadly. Accusation could be brought by anyone, including people such as women, slaves, *infames* and freedmen, who were normally debarred. Torture could be applied not only to slaves (which was compulsory) but also to free men, excluding senators (D. 48.4.7–8). As proceedings before the Senate were flexible, in that they did not require a previous selection of court, any dubious behaviour could be brought within its judicial remit, so that it is not always possible to identify the charge precisely. Libo Drusus, a silly young man according to Tacitus, was accused before the Senate in 16 of 'plotting revolution', because allegedly magic arts had been used to threaten the safety of leading men (Vell. Pat. 2.129–30; Tac. *Ann.* 2.27–32; Suet. *Tib.* 25; Dio 57.15.4–6; Rutledge 2001: 159–61, 232). Evidence consisted of allegations that Libo had consulted a fortune-teller and, crucially, a list of names of prominent people with mysterious markings attached. He anticipated the verdict by suicide (Tac. *Ann.* 2.27–32). It was also possible to supplement another public charge with one of *maiestas*; Silanus, former governor of Asia, was prosecuted by the province under the *repetundae* statute, but his defence was hamstrung by the addition of a treason charge, which effectively silenced such friends as he had (Tac. *Ann.* 4.65–9).

Treason under the Empire is mostly heard of as a senatorial crime, and blame for the abuse of the charge is laid at the doors of emperors, their agents, or the 'informers' (*delatores*) who exploited the system for personal gain (Rutledge 2001: 20–53; Rivière 2002). But Tacitus, at least, was clear that the senators themselves were the main culprits, acting as informers on each other, inventing some ludicrous slants on the law and even advancing their careers thereby; the prominent *delator*, Fulcinius Trio (Rutledge 2001: 234–5), who prosecuted Libo Drusus, went on to hold the suffect consulship in July 31. Past practice validated the actions of Senate and *princeps* in more ways than one. Prosecutions were exploited as a cover for senatorial competition, for the elimination of rivals. The resulting precedents were created out of political conflict – without concern or thought for legal principle – by an elite out of control.

But the treason law was also a means by which the elite was brought under increasingly stringent control by an ever more overt autocracy. How far it was formally used in the second century AD is uncertain. In 117, on the accession of Hadrian, four senators were summarily executed in different locations for their alleged participation in a conspiracy to murder the new emperor. Such conspiracy was clearly *maiestas* but there was no formal process other than a vote of the Senate in their absence, which Hadrian, after the event, piously deplored, claiming he had not wished for their deaths (*SHA Hadrian* 7). The Senate's main worry in the age of the Antonines was that they might be exposed to summary execution; emperors regularly assured senators that they would not execute a senator without taking a vote. Severus, notoriously, was quick to execute the very senator who had jointly proposed a decree to that effect on his accession in 193 (Dio 75.2.2). Severus, patron of the greatest Roman jurists and a legalist when it suited him, adroitly combined law with terror. As the senatorial observer

Dio wryly commented after a purge in 205, ' he killed many other senators, *some of whom* had been formally accused, pleaded their case and been condemned' (Dio, *Epitome* 77.7.3).

TREASON IN LATE ANTIQUITY

The Theodosian Code (compiled 429–37) is not the place to look for a comprehensive definition of treason – although the mistaken belief that this was its purpose would cost one imperial official dear (Sidonius, *Letter* 1.7, see below, p. 83). Its contents do, however, represent the outcome of several hundred years of combining *maiestas* with other crimes. Most bizarre is the choice of the compilers to list in the section on the Lex Cornelia on assassins and poisoners a constitution of 397 about criminal conspiracy, and threats to the lives of imperial councillors, senators and administrators (*CT* 9.14.3); the compilers of Justinian's Code sensibly reinstated it under the Lex Julia *maiestatis* (*CJ* 9.8.5). The situation addressed by the law was one of potential revolt against the emperor Arcadius in Constantinople, which was treason by any definition. The content and phrasing are consistent with the law of treason, which applied to those plotting to harm magistrates and holders of *imperium*. Punishment for these murderous plots was to be 'executed as one guilty of *maiestas*', along with confiscation of all property (cf. *CT* 9.42.2–6; 8.3; 23; *CT* 10.10.15). The sons of the traitors would have their lives spared, as a demonstration of imperial clemency, but their rights to inherit from anyone or to hold office were severely curtailed. Women, being 'less bold on account of the weakness of their sex', were permitted the legal minimum inheritance from their mothers. Anyone who interceded for the traitors would be branded with infamy.

This represents the most prominent illustration of the Theodosian Code's habit of including *maiestas* under other headings than its governing statute; as we have it, the Lex Julia *maiestatis* chapter contains only one law, a procedural reform of Constantine, which made accusers in treason trials also liable to torture if their cases lacked supporting testimony (*CT* 9.5.1). *Maiestas* is in fact omnipresent in the Code, in two guises, as 'treason' (but not under the right heading) or as offences to be treated as if treason. Imperial legislators required space to exercise discretion. Verbal abuse of emperors might not always be treasonable, if, for example, the abuser was drunk, light-headed or insane, therefore each such case should be considered on its merits (*CT* 9.4). Crimes identified as equivalent to treason (and therefore to be added to the ever-growing list contained in the Lex Julia, senatorial precedents and imperial decisions) included the incarceration of accused people in private prisons (*CT* 9.11.1, of 388); counterfeiting of imperial coinage (*CT* 9.21.9, of 392); the illegal use of purple dye, after some three hundred pounds of illicitly dyed purple silk went on public sale (*CT* 10.20.18, of 436; cf. *CT* 10.21.3, of 424); and the inscribing of their own names by governors on public works, rather than that of the emperor (*CT* 15.1.31.pr.).

The procedures and penalties were as stern as they had been under the Principate. The late third-century author of Paulus' *Sententiae*, having explained that formerly the punishment for treason was interdiction from fire and water, informed his readers that 'nowadays', members of the lower classes were thrown to the beasts or burned alive, while their betters, the *honestiores*, suffered capital punishment (Paulus, *Sent.* 5.29). The Augustan precedent, set in 22 BC by the executions of Caepio and Murena, had become the norm. Exemptions from torture on grounds of status did not apply to *maiestas* cases, although leading senators in 370 succeeded in reasserting senatorial immunity, after it had been eroded by the activities of Valentinian I's henchman at Rome (Amm. Marc. 28.1.24-5; Matthews 1989: 212–18). As so often, emperors, especially those temperamentally inclined to cruelty, failed to check over-zealous subordinates. In the course of Valentinian's purge of senators in *c.* 370, the slaves of one Aginatius, who was accused of unlawful sex (*stuprum*) but not treason, were tortured until one uttered an ambiguous confession, even though 'our most merciful laws forbid this from happening in a case of *stuprum*' (Amm. Marc. 28.1.54). Those condemned had no hope of relief; along with murderers, poisoners, magicians, adulterers, rapists and those guilty of crimes against the dead, the traitor could not hope to benefit from amnesties at Eastertide (*CT* 9.38.3-4; 6).

It was always the case that *perduellio/maiestas* was the worst of crimes, because the traitor endangered the security of the whole community. It was therefore expected that the punishment should be exceptional, that all should be empowered to inform if all might be put at risk, that all measures, including torture of anyone, regardless of status, were legitimate if the security of the community was to be safeguarded. But if the fear was overdone, the result could be the subversion of the values of the community, which the treason law was supposed to protect. When the emperor Valens discovered in 371 that a group of philosophers at Antioch had been holding a series of séances to find out the name of the next emperor, he panicked and resorted to torture of numerous suspects, who proceeded to implicate each other and yet more innocent people as well (Amm. Marc.

29.1.5–38; Matthews 1989: 219–22). 'His monstrous savagery spread everywhere like a burning torch and was fanned by the servile flattery of many,' wrote Ammianus, a personal observer of events and a native of the city; 'in his despotic rage, he was quick to attack the guilty and innocent alike with malicious prosecution under one and the same law . . .' Thus the fate of the accused depended 'not on the truth but on the nod of one man'. Like Tacitus, whose work he continued, Ammianus saw abuse of the treason law as equivalent to the suspension of all law. The outcome of the trials was consistent; the accused were executed in one batch, unlawfully, by a single decree.

While the security of the Empire was not in fact at risk from outside enemies, the application of the *perduellio* interpretation of treason mattered less than the emperor's (and his courtiers') obsession with his (and their) own security and status. The Theodosian Code's obsession with purple dye and suchlike reflects that sense of priorities. However, the offences covered by *perduellio* remained in force. In 469 the twice praetorian prefect of Gaul, Arvandus, was brought to trial before the Senate by the provincial council of the Gauls (Sidonius, *Letter* 1.7; Harries 1992; 1994: 159–66). Ostensibly the charge was extortion but the wily delegates exploited the flexibility of senatorial procedures to ambush the defendant with a charge of *maiestas*, on the grounds that he had 'treasonably' corresponded with the Gothic king, Euric, and offered to hand over large parts of Gaul to his rule. As the letter was dictated, Arvandus could have denied the charge on grounds of forgery. Instead, foolishly, he admitted authorship of the letter 'forgetting', as one observer put it, that treason was not confined to offences against the emperor. The senators at Rome, being more conversant with Roman legal tradition, had no hesitation in pronouncing a guilty verdict.

CONCLUSION

The law of *maiestas* is perhaps best understood as the uneasy combination of two separate strands of thought on the meaning of treason. The first, which we may call *perduellio*, relates directly to the security of the community and seeks to punish those who damage it by helping enemies, launching attacks on their own country or people, seeking to murder political and other leaders or subverting the constitution and the laws. The second is the idea of damage to, or diminution of, not the security of the people, but its 'greatness' – a concept which defies definition. To be guilty of *maiestas*, in the sense conceived first by Saturninus, it was not necessary to have threatened the security of the community or collaborated with enemies. Legally, it became possible to prosecute for actions which had no bearing whatever on national security, or even that of the emperor and his associates.

Not that the Romans were unique in the flexibility they ascribed to treason. Even a casual glance through the catalogues of one university library reveals book titles which accuse their subjects of 'treason', from various perspectives, among them Judas and the Antichrist (the latter for 'treason against God'), Louis XVI of France, J. Edgar Hoover (for his alleged responsibility for the assassination of President Kennedy) and American Liberals. It has also been acceptable to expand the definition of treason by statute: in 1793 an act was passed 'declaring it high treason to counterfeit His Majesty's seal of this province' (Georgia, USA – Emory Microfiche 41344). Insulting the sovereign could also count as treason, even when the speaker was a relatively humble individual: in the seventeenth century one William Stayley, a goldsmith, was convicted 'for speaking treasonable words against his most sacred majesty'.

Ancient writers were not interested in traitors of modest means and status, partly because misbehaviour on their part would inflict less damage. Few would have disagreed with the need for a *perduellio* law to punish those who harmed national security. But the application of the *maiestas* law, throughout its history, was dogged by controversy. Created at a time of political turbulence, the Lex Appuleia *maiestatis* was aimed at the perceived enemies of the people, an attempt to control the less 'popular' elements in the ruling elite. Its lack of definition made it a useful tool in political rivalries, as pursued through the criminal courts. Its abuse led to serious attempts by Sulla and later Caesar to establish outline rules and definitions, helped by the assimilation of the more rigorously perceived offences classed historically as *perduellio*.

Greed for rewards on the part of informers, senatorial sycophancy exhibited at the conviction, however unjust, of the emperor's enemies, and fear of challenging autocracy underlay the exploitation of *maiestas* in the reigns of Tiberius and other emperors, whose indifference or insecurity allowed the abuse of prosecution to flourish. Tacitus' account may be overdone, influenced by experience under Domitian (and guilt at having survived the reign). So too may be Ammianus' impatience with the suspicious fears of Constantius II (reigning Augustus 337–61; Matthews 1989: 34–40), Valentinian I and Valens. But the fact remains that there were senatorial and other conspiracies against emperors, some of them (such as those against Caligula in 41, Domitian in 96 and Commodus in 192) successful. There were also army revolts: Constantius' own brother had succumbed to military challenge in Gaul in 350, and he died of an illness, aged 44, while marching to meet a further rebel, his cousin the Caesar Julian. Unpredictable though it was, lacking in definition and open to abuse, a treason law was necessary for emperors to justify the measures they took for their own protection against their soldiers, their governing class and even their supposed friends. Only at the very end of Roman rule in the West did the ruling elite at Rome recall that its purpose was to protect national security as well.

CHAPTER 7

Sex and the City

If law is viewed as an instrument of social control, its content and its efficacy will depend on its relationship to social customs and institutions, not least those which define the social meanings of sex and gender: 'men and women are both controlled by such mechanisms as the family, marriage, work and concepts of "masculinity" and "femininity"' (Morris 1987: 17). The early Roman community (which did not have the separate identity implied by the word 'state') was built around the family and household, headed by the *paterfamilias*, the eldest male ascendant, with his absolute legal jurisdiction, including the power of life and death (*ius vitae necisque*), over his descendants. Its religious character and continuity was expressed in its *sacra*, which further identified the family as part of the community as religious construct.

In this system a woman's control of her own body was subordinate to that of her family, of birth and then of marriage. Her function was to provide children; remaining single was, for most, not an option, until the advent of Christianity. Their marriages were arranged by their *paterfamilias*, as were those of their brothers, but the consent of the parties was also a requirement (Treggiari 1991: 170–80). In *manus*-marriage a woman became subject to the legal power of her husband, as if he were her father; in non-*manus* marriage she remained under the power of her father and a member, for religious and legal purposes, of his household (1991: 16–34). If the marriage was unhappy the wife could make her voice heard by complaining (as Cicero's sister-in-law was known to do) or by seeking divorce, but domestic abuse was seldom acknowledged to exist and could even be praised (Val. Max. 6.3.9), if the wife provided an excuse by behaving badly (contrast the current slogan advertised by the Scottish Executive: 'Domestic Abuse: There's No Excuse'). To violate or seduce a woman of family was to dishonour her family (Pliny, *Letter* 6.31; D. 48.6.5.2; McGinn 1998: 10–14). Thus the abductor of a woman and the woman herself were punished whether or not the woman had actually consented, as it was assumed that she could have prevented it, had she wished; punishment was inflicted even if the father had forgiven the wrong done to him (Evans Grubbs 1989; 1995: 183–93). The law acknowledged the claims of honour but was less receptive to those of forgiveness or of love.

ABORTION

In law, legitimate children were the property of their *paterfamilias* from conception onwards. When considering abortion, therefore, the legal discourse, which first emerged in the Severan period, took account only of the father's rights, and abortion was a crime against the father, for which in the third century the penalty was exile (D. 47.11.4; 48.8.8). At the start of the fourth century Paulus' *Sententiae* prescribed the mines for humbler folk and retained exile, plus confiscation of goods, for the better classes, with the proviso that the death penalty would apply if someone died (D. 48.19.38.5). The Severan jurist Tryphoninus referred back to Cicero's story (*Clu.* 32) of the woman of Miletus who was executed for performing an abortion for financial gain; he added that exile would also be the fate of women who had aborted after divorce because of their hatred of the father (D. 48.19.39). All this does not imply that abortion was 'legal' before Severus issued his rescript (D. 47.11.4) on the matter. Disposing of a husband's child without his authority was to deprive him of his property, and social, if not legal, penalties would have inevitably followed.

Legal discourse, unlike that of philosophy or Christianity (Dickison 1973), did not consider the 'right to life' of the foetus. Nor was it concerned with the risks to the mother of continuing a dangerous pregnancy. In these areas the concerns of the law contrast (and could well have clashed) with those of gynaecologists. Writing in the first century AD, Soranus recorded two schools of thought (*Gyn.* 1.60). One, which continued the 'Hippocratic' tradition, insisted that abortion was never acceptable, because it was the task of medicine to 'safeguard and preserve what has been engendered by nature'. The other allowed abortion in certain restricted circumstances if the mother's life was threatened by the further development of the foetus, because her womb was too small or malformed. The doctors would not condone abortion of the offspring of adultery or for reasons of vanity.

Literature provides a third, if not entirely sympathetic, perspective. Juvenal castigated the wealthy for infidelity and vanity; echoing the medical writers, he maintained that abortions were to preserve the figure or conceal the fruits of adultery (*Sat.* 6.592–600) and neither motive was acceptable. In a mannered but more nuanced fashion Ovid rehearsed the arguments for and against an abortion which threatened the life of the mother. His (literary) seduction of a married woman, Corinna, is complicated by her 'rash' decision to abort her unborn child, with disastrous physical consequences. In two poems the poet acknowledges the importance of the lives of both mother and child, but not, perhaps understandably, the rights of the (cuckolded) husband or father. *Amores* 2.13 is a straightforward prayer to Isis and the goddess of childbirth to spare Corinna's life, a theme reprised in the last lines of *Amores* 2.14. However, 2.14 as a whole offers a more critical account of Corinna's motives, adducing the fear of stretch-marks (2.14.7) and expressing revulsion at the 'poisoning' and mauling of the foetus by surgical instruments (2.14.27–8); even wild animals cherish their young (2.14.35–6). Although in the last four lines the poet-lover relents, praying that she may be punished – but not yet, he also concedes the social abhorrence of a mother who, in effect, kills her child. If she died herself as a result, the bystanders at her funeral would merely observe, 'served her right' (2.14.39–40). Though in many respects artificial, Ovid is witness to a powerful social and moral discourse on abortion, which is not reflected in the law and which did concede the rights of the child (as Christianity was also to do) – even while the poet himself is more concerned with the fate of the mistress-mother.

RAPE

Rape was a public crime, because it was termed 'fornication by force' (*stuprum per vim*) and therefore counted as *vis publica* (D. 48.6.3.4). Those intimidated by the threat of sexual assault could also seek redress by civil means, through actions for *metus* (fear). Roman law, unlike some systems, did not blame the woman, provided that she was of respectable status. Because she had not consented to intercourse, her reputation did not suffer and, if not married, her chances of marriage, in law, were unaffected (Ulpian at D. 48.5.14(13).7). Social attitudes were surprisingly mixed. The stage treatment of sexual violation argues some insensitivity to the trauma of rape on the part of authors and audiences. Rape in early Roman Comedy was a plot device, sometimes traumatic for the victim at the time, but all was made well when the ravisher and his victim married or turned out to be married already (Scafuro 1997: 216–18, 226–8). Some readings of Ovid in particular argue that the poet exploited legendary rapes as a form of sexual titillation for his readers (Richlin 1981).

The moral tradition of Rome passed down stories of how the rights of even prostitutes to resist rape could be safeguarded by the authorities. In the mid second century BC the aedile Hostilius Mancinus tried to force his way into the house of a prostitute, Manilia, who responded by pelting him with stones; when he tried to sue her for throwing stones at him, the tribunes refused to hear the case (Gell. *NA* 4.14; McGinn 1998: 60–1, 327; cf. Sen. *Controv.* 1.2). But other sources suggest that actresses in particular had few means of self-defence, as they were assumed to be sexually available. Cicero accepted the gang-rape of a *mima* at Atina as part of local custom (*Planc.* 30) – although he also insisted that his client was innocent of that too – and, four hundred years later, the authorities penalised the abductor of an actress with a fine of five pounds of gold, not for the injury to her, but because he had robbed the public of their entertainment (*CT* 15.7.5, of 380).

LAW AND MORALITY

In the dominant ideology of the Augustan period, which reacted against the more liberated lifestyles of the circles of Catullus, Clodia and later Antonius, Propertius and Ovid by drawing on traditions from earlier centuries, the body of a woman was at the service of her family and of the state. Livy's model women acquiesced in or even asserted their role as vessels of honour. When the silent Verginia became the object of Appius Claudius' licentious desires, her family was saved from dishonour by her father, who killed her with a butcher's knife (Livy 3.45). Lucretia preferred suicide to surviving the dishonour inflicted on her husband, Collatinus, by her rape (Livy 1.57.6–58). For both, the preservation of the purity or chastity of the woman matters more than her life. In the case of Lucretia the story gains added point, as the exemplary *matrona* insists on killing herself, despite her husband's adherence to the legal position (in Livy's day) that she had not consented and was therefore innocent. The Livian stories were a part of Augustus' moral message. Women were expected actively to support the honour system, not merely to acquiesce in it.

In matters sexual the law is frequently found in conflict with other forms of discourse. What the law, at least from 18 BC onwards, penalised as *stuprum*, unlawful sex, or *adulterium*, sex between a married woman and a lover, was for some poets the source of their inspiration and for others (the numbers are unquantifiable) an accepted lifestyle. Illicit love inspired ingenious legal dodges: the emperor Tiberius was obliged to forbid one Vistilia, a respectable married woman, from acquiring immunity from the adultery law by registering on the aedile's list as a prostitute (Tac. *Ann.* 2.85). The affair provoked a senatorial resolution that a woman who became a brothel madam or an actress to avoid a charge of adultery could nonetheless be charged (D. 48.5.11(10).2). The decree was a recognition of the social limits of the law: to be charged, one had to have some kind of status in the first place. In the fourth century AD Constantine, himself the son of a tavern waitress, re-enacted the rule that the mistress of a tavern counted as a *materfamilias* and so could be liable, but the waitresses were not: 'chastity is required only of those women who are held by the bond of law but those who, because of their lowly status in life, are not considered worthy of the consideration of the laws shall be safe from judicial severity' (*CT* 9.7.1).

INCESTUM

Adultery, therefore, was a contested area. So too, for different reasons, was *incestum*, which carried two distinct meanings. One was sex with a Vestal Virgin, which brought pollution on the community and even endangered its safety; the second was marriage between people so closely related that the law denied them the *ius conubii*, the right to be married and have legitimate children (Robinson 1995: 154–7; Evans Grubbs 2002: 136–43). While incest, in the second sense, might be expected to provoke extreme social disapproval, Rome's acquisition of an Empire, which included such endogamous communities as those that existed in Egypt, resulted in a more restrained approach to 'marriage' between relations, focusing on legal disability rather than religious pollution.

The verb *incesto* signifies religious and/or sexual pollution, such as that created by the presence of a corpse (Virg. *Aen.* 6.150), or the seduction of a Vestal Virgin or Christian nun (*TLL* 892–3). Early Roman religious sanctions reflected social abhorrence of sex between close kin or of unnatural sexual practices in general (Suet. *Tib.* 43.1). In all its forms *incestum* combined two ideas: that of religious pollution (*piaculum*, cf. Tac. *Ann.* 12.8.2), which could be beyond expiation if, for example, it entailed the loss of a sacred virginity; and that of immorality or shamelessness. The social taboo against *incestum* was activated against wrongdoers through Rome's earliest religious laws (*leges sacratae*), which, like the later *publica iudicia*, were part of Roman public law. If those involved in a religious cult could be implicated in charges of incest, they faced possible legal sanction and certain social isolation. Cicero described as *incestum* Clodius' attempt to have sex with the wife of the Pontifex Maximus at an all-female religious festival (*Pis.* 95); his ideal code of religious law gave his *pontifices* the power to inflict the death sentence for *incestum* (*Leg.* 2.22, cf. 2.41).

Sex between close kin violated Roman religious and social convention, and allegations of impropriety provided material for political and forensic invective. Cicero's attacks on Clodius in the 50s were regularly adorned with snide asides about his alleged sexual relationship with his sister. In a conversation on religion between a pagan and a Christian 'recorded' by Minucius Felix in the second century, accusations of incest are made by both parties against the other. The pagan (Min. Fel. *Octavius* 9.7) claims that all Christians are tainted with incest if not by deed but by their guilty consciences (deriving from Christians' calling each other brother and sister); the Christian retaliates by pointing out the incestuous nature of the pagan gods, who mate with their mother, daughter or sister (*Octavius* 31.3, cf. Tertullian, *Apologeticus* 9.16). Even when the civil penalties attached to incest are under discussion, the terminology reflects social distaste: incestuous marriages are 'contrary to right' (*nefariae*, Gaius, *Inst.* 1.59 and 64; cf. Marcian at D. 40.18.5, *incestum* as *contra fas*).

Incestum in a religious context incurred the anger of the gods and therefore threatened the security of all. If a Vestal Virgin lost her virginity to a seducer, religious pollution was brought on the whole community and the penalty was death, in accordance with prescribed ritual. This was supervised by the Pontifex Maximus, who was in charge of the six Vestals from the time of their recruitment, perhaps aged as young as six, for the thirty years of their office. The seducer was beaten to death by the Pontifex Maximus in the Forum (Livy 22.57.3; Suet. *Dom.* 8.5; Plin. *Letter.* 4.11; Plut. *Numa* 10). The former Virgin was escorted, in what may have represented a funeral procession, to the Campus Sceleratus, the Plain of Wickedness, near the Colline Gate, where she was buried alive (Fraschetti 1984). The exact rationale for the process is obscure (Cornell 1981). The Pontifex Maximus had jurisdiction over all priests and had a formal, almost 'paternal', authority over the Vestals (Beard 1980, 1994). The Vestals were required to be free from bodily defect. Loss of virginity was inexpiable, not only because it was irreversible but also because it was deliberately incurred (cf. Varro, *De lingua Latina* 6.30; Macrobius, *Saturnalia* 1.16.10). On these religious as well as legal grounds, the Vestal Virgin was 'as if' dead from the moment her virginity was lost, hence the (funeral) procession and the entombment.

In early Rome the connection between unlawful sex and national calamity does not appear to have been openly challenged. Livy's account of one delinquent explains that suspicion was aroused by the Vestal

Minucia's showy attire (Livy 8.15.8). She was denounced before the *pon-tifices* by a slave and ordered by their decree to abstain from the *sacra*, while keeping the slave in her own *potestas*, pending the trial. The pontifical hearing and condemnation duly followed. But confusion between cause and effect was clearly possible. When the Romans were massively defeated at Cannae by Hannibal in 216 BC, it was taken for granted that the gods were offended; an impure Vestal was duly detected and entombed.

But accusations of incest with a Vestal Virgin could also be influenced by politics combined with religious hysteria (Rawson 1974). In 114 BC, the Romans suffered a disastrous defeat by a Thracian tribe, the Scordisci. In December of that year three Vestal Virgins, Aemilia, Licinia and Marcia, that is, half the college, were tried by the Pontifex Maximus, but only one was condemned. Early in 113 a special *quaestio* was set up under the presidency of one L. Cassius (Asc. *Mil.* 46C), who tried the two Vestals again and found them guilty; they were then executed but not entombed (Plut. *Quaest. Rom.* 83; Oros. 5.15.20–1). One of their alleged lovers was M. Antonius, later consul and a leading (fictitious) participant in Cicero's dialogue *De oratore*; he was tried in 113 but acquitted (Val. Max. 3.7.9; Gruen 1968b).

Under the Empire the need to protect the unpolluted hearth of Vesta appears to have been less acutely felt; even under Augustus there were recruitment problems, which evoked from the emperor the pledge that he would have offered one of his own descendants – if he had had one of the right age. But Domitian (Augustus 81–96) had other ideas (Bauman 1996: 92–9). In 83 he tried three Vestals for unchastity under secular process and allowed them to choose the manner of their death (Suet. *Dom.* 8.3–4; Dio 67.3.4). Six years later he invoked the religious penalty against the chief Vestal, Cornelia. Pliny vigorously condemned her conviction by Domitian, recalling her distress as she was led to execution and how, as she descended into the tomb, she even refused the executioner's help with her robe, because she so consistently had rejected the touch of men (*Letter* 4.11). Part of his motivation was enmity towards Domitian, who he claimed was guilty of incest himself; but he clearly also believed that Cornelia was framed, despite Domitian's self-justifying production of a confession from the alleged lover, whose plea bargaining had allowed him escape into exile.

For Dio, Pliny and Suetonius, religious issues were clearly of secondary importance. Whatever Domitian's real 'moral agenda', persecution of the Vestals was read as symptomatic of his character as a 'bad' emperor. The same applies to Dio's censure of Caracalla's wholesale condemnation of four Vestal Virgins, three of whom were buried alive, while one anticipated execution by throwing herself from the roof (Dio 78.16.1). While this may have related to an attempt to revive the cult of Vesta, Caracalla's behaviour is construed as both harsh and hypocritical; like Domitian, he exploited the Vestals to distract attention from his own perversions (or, allegedly, impotence). But, for religious conservatives, they would remain a symbol to the end. In the late fourth century there was controversy over the sentencing to death (but not live burial) of the Vestal Primigenia, who was found guilty of *incestum* by the Pontiffs (although there was no longer an imperial Pontifex Maximus); the Prefect of the City refused to co-operate with the execution, on the pretext that Alba, where the offence happened, was outside his jurisdiction (Symm. *Letters* 9.147–8).

Sex on the part of a Vestal Virgin, therefore, was a religious delict, punishable by the religious authorities. In Roman society in general, although not, as we shall see, in all the provinces, sex and marriage with close relations were viewed with distaste. However, the 'criminal' status of sex and marriage within the forbidden degrees is uncertain, though accepted by Robinson (1995: 54). Augustus' law against adulteries also encompassed *stuprum*, but is not known explicitly to have included incest. Tiberius executed Sex. Marius, the richest man in Spain, for having sex with his own daughter, by hurling him from the Tarpeian Rock. Tacitus maintained that it was a frame-up, in order to seize Marius' money (*Ann.* 6.19.1), and no reference is made to Augustan precedent or authority. But Tiberius' action would provide an imperial precedent for punishing incest with the death penalty as a 'criminal' offence.

In the late second century Papinian discussed the 'question' of what happened when incest was combined with adultery, a situation which could well have arisen, given that for many women their main social contacts would be with other members of their own family. Papinian argued (D. 48.5.39(38).2) that if unlawful sex (*stuprum*) took place between a man and his sister's daughter, and the woman thought, mistakenly, that this was permissible, her ignorance should count as her excuse; presumably she might know of the precedent which legalised the marriage of the Emperor Claudius and his brother's daughter, Agrippina (Tac. *Ann.* 12.6–7; Gaius, *Inst.* 1.62), but be unaware that this did not extend to daughters of sisters. She should suffer the same penalty as men, Papinian wrote, only when she is found guilty of incest prohibited under universal law (*iure gentium*) – which, it is implied, she should have known about. If, he continued, the question concerned only observance of Roman citizen law (*ius civile*), the woman would not be charged with incest, although if incest had been combined with adultery, the adultery charge would stand.

There did exist, therefore, a *crimen*, a criminal charge, of incest, based perhaps on the Tiberian precedent, social disapproval of sex between close kin, and assimilation of incest to unlawful sex in general, as outlawed by the Lex Julia on adulteries.

However, the main concentration of juristic writing on incest concerns the legal status of the 'incestuous' marriage under the civil law, which is discussed in the 'edictal' Digest 23. Paulus in the late second or early third century provided a definition of incest: 'if anyone marries a person from the types of relations whom we are forbidden by custom (*moribus*) to marry, he is said to have committed incest' (D. 23.2.39). 'Custom' in this context refers to 'customary law', which is binding on the citizen. However, it also allows for local variants, such as the practice of brother–sister marriage, hallowed by centuries of usage in Roman Egypt. If Roman citizens entered on an incestuous marriage, they were liable only to the civil consequences of not being properly married, that is their children counted as illegitimate; they belonged to their mother, which meant that they did not have the rights, protection or duties of being subject to *patria potestas*, and they were debarred from inheriting. For families with little property, these sanctions may have had little effect. Far more of a deterrent would have been social disapproval of unions which were against 'natural law and modesty (*pudor*)' (Paulus, D. 23.2.14.2).

Incestuous sex and marriage were offences against the moral order established by mankind in general through the *ius gentium* but defined more specifically by Roman law. In Late Antiquity the civil-law tradition continued to be observed but was occasionally overwhelmed by the moralistic priorities of emperors. Diocletian, in an edict published in 295, expressed imperial revulsion at incest, before going on to restate the forbidden degrees of relationship, warning those who continued in their unlawful marriages about the legal disabilities which threatened their descendants (*Collatio* 6.4.1; cf. 6.5.1; Evans Grubbs 2002: 140–3). Despite the aggressive rhetoric, this was a reinforcement of the civil tradition. However, by the 340s Christian disapproval of sexual irregularities in general prompted Constans and Constantius II to threaten the incestuously married with capital punishment (*CT* 3.12.1). Religious abhorrence of incest and the influence of Ambrose of Milan may have influenced Gratian and later Valentinian II to exempt the incestuous from Easter amnesties, along with parricides, murderers, adulterers, sorcerers and traitors (*CT* 9.38.6, of 381; 9.38.8, of 385). However, by the end of the century the Eastern imperial court, more conversant with the legal tradition, revoked the capital penalties on the incestuous imposed by previous emperors but continued public condemnation of the 'pollution' of incestuous marriages, retaining civil financial penalties and testamentary restrictions for the offenders and their children (*CT* 3.12.3.8, of 396).

Incestum is one of the more complex offences against the Roman social order. By definition, it caused religious pollution. The unchaste Vestal and her lover were removed from the community by ritual means, authorised and implemented by the religious authorities. Unlawful sex between family members, whose relationship denied them the *ius conubii*, was liable to both social stigma and legal sanction. Because *incestum* was a loaded term in public discourse, it could be exploited in the service of political invective against opponents, or as a general reproach, and because it carried religious pollution, it could be seriously damaging when levelled against a suspect religion or cult. But the rulers of an Empire which contained endogamous societies could not legally proscribe whole communities. Therefore Roman social values were expressed through the civil disabilities attached to incestuous marriages and, increasingly, the imperial rhetoric of moral censure – which could, on occasion, translate into criminal prosecution and punishment as well.

THE LEX JULIA ON ADULTERIES AND UNLAWFUL SEX

Adultery existed before Augustus made it a public crime in 18 BC. It was punished by the family, which had the choice whether or not to take action. It was recorded, much later, that Romulus had legislated against women who poisoned their husband's children, counterfeited his keys or committed adultery (Plut. *Rom.* 25). Cato the Censor, whose stern views of morality were proverbial, stated that a wronged husband had the right both to judge the morals of his wife and to execute her, punishing her for being drunk and killing her for infidelity (Cato, *On Dowries*, cited by Aulus Gellius, *NA* 10.23.4–5). A husband's control of his wife's actions extended, in Roman tradition, to divorce on grounds of going outside with the head uncovered, talking privately to a freedwoman or attending the games without telling the husband first (Val. Max. 6.3; 10–12).

The Lex Julia on adulteries should be seen in the context of Augustus' broader interest in families in general, and his belief, which was controversial, that it was appropriate for the community as legislator to take an interest in their behaviour. Augustus required Roman citizen families to behave in the public interest. He legislated to encourage the production of children and, in the Lex Papia Poppaea, penalised celibacy by restricting the ability of the childless to benefit from wills (Suet. *Aug.* 34); according to

Tacitus, the only beneficiaries of this were informers (Tac. *Ann.* 3.25 and 28). He also clarified, in the Lex Julia *de maritandis ordinibus*, what counted as legal marriage between the orders, for the production of legitimate children. His concern with the fertility of Romans had Republican precedent: a speech of Metellus Macedonicus in 131 had advocated the production of more Roman citizens, and Augustus quoted it with approval (Livy, *Per.* 59). However, it was one thing to deliver a speech, and quite another to interfere in the long-established operation of the authority of a *paterfamilias* over his household.

Adultery was defined as sex between a married woman and a man not her husband; his marital status was immaterial. This damaged the family – and thus the community – in two ways. First it made it possible for a child to be imported into a household and acknowledged by a *pater* who was not the *pater*'s biological child – hence the etymology of the word offered by Papinian (D. 48.5.6.1) as 'child conceived by another' (*partum ab alio conceptum*). Once acknowledged, it succeeded to all the rights of an heir on the *pater*'s death. Secondly, and no less important, adultery damaged family honour, which was vested in the womenfolk and safeguarded by the men. Part of the father's or husband's role, therefore, was to adjudicate on suspected adultery and punish the offending member of the family and it was up to them what action, if any, to take.

The Lex Julia on adulteries was, therefore, a significant expansion of outside regulation into a domain jealously guarded by the family, and the *paterfamilias* in particular. It introduced new thinking on what was 'criminal' in the sense of being a threat to the public good. What consenting adults did in private was made the concern of the community. From Augustus' standpoint, his programme of social and moral renewal required that the public authorities concerned themselves with the moral standards of the citizens as a whole; the traditional role of the censor as supervisor of morals provided precedent. The challenge, therefore, which faced his legal draftsmen was the defining of new boundaries between the *res publica* and familial competence in the protection of honour, morals and the bloodline.

The section in the Digest which collects juristic interpretation of the Lex Julia (D. 48.5) provides an object lesson in how to read that problematic collection. The text of the Lex Julia seems to have survived exceptionally well, as a number of clauses are quoted directly and the author is named. It is also exceptional in that it generated a number of juristic commentaries in the Severan period devoted specifically to adultery. This broke with the previous mode of discourse, which was to treat the *publica iudicia* together. No other public offence merited such emphasis, and it has been suggested that the treatises on adultery were composed to mark the formal abolition of the *quaestio* on adulteries at Rome by Septimius Severus or Caracalla, and the transfer of its business to the jurisdiction of the Prefect of the City (Bauman 1968, against Garnsey 1967).

There are thus two layers of discussion of adultery and unlawful sex present in the Digest, with over two hundred years between them. To this should be added the effects of the selection process engaged in by Justinian's compilers in the early 530s, which create the misleading impression of a unified discourse, effortlessly informing the reader 'what the law was'. The historian of legal and social culture, however, is best advised to treat the collection as a set of fragmentary texts (the jurists) containing within them further fragments (of the law); the compilers would have had the full texts of the commentaries, if not the law, before them and would have therefore already censored the material available.

The Lex Julia *de adulteriis* (in general, see Bauman 1996: 34–6) may have opened with a declaration of intent: the 'words of the statute' were 'let no one hereafter and with malicious intent commit adultery or *stuprum*' (D. 48.5.13(12)). In the second clause (Paulus, *Sent.* 2.26.1) Augustus addressed and effectively limited the rights of fathers, who had the full rights of *patresfamilias*, and husbands to kill daughters or wives and their lovers. Greater powers were granted to the father of a daughter *in potestate* (i.e. married without *manus*), provided that certain conditions were met. He could kill his daughter-in-power and her lover, provided that they were caught in the act and that both were killed immediately or very soon after (D. 48.5.21(20)pr., and 2; 48.5.24(23)pr. and 4). The location where the right could be exercised was restricted to the house (or 'domicile') of the father, even if the daughter no longer lived there, or of the husband. It followed that if the lovers were killed elsewhere, or if only one of them was killed, an action for homicide could be brought under the Lex Cornelia *de sicariis* (D. 48.5.33(32)).

At or around clause 5 (D. 48.5.26(25)) the rights of the husband over the apprehended adulterer were set out. Many lovers, though caught in a compromising situation, could not lawfully be killed. The offenders must be caught in the act and in the husband's own house; he could not take action if the adultery had happened in the house of his father-in-law. The husband could summarily kill the lover only if he were a man of low social class, a procurer, actor, dancer or convict, or freedman of the husband or various of his relatives (D. 48.5.25(24)pr.). The wife was then to be divorced at once.

The early clauses of the law intruded on the ancient rights of fathers of children *in potestate* to inflict the death penalty at will. However, the status of the statute in relation to the ancient *ius vitae necisque* is uncertain (McGinn 1998: 203–6). By the time of Augustus the power of life and death may have fallen into abeyance, allowing the statute to invoke the power of present customary practice when imposing formal limits on family executions for adultery. Moreover, limited permission to kill was granted to all fathers, whether they were themselves 'in-power' or not; the biological fact was more relevant in this context than legal status. This, together with the provision allowing summary killing of low-class lovers, suggests that the law was sensitive to considerations of honour; betrayal of a husband with, say, a mime-actor was clearly an exceptionally grave infringement. But the provisions relating to location and the catching of the couple *in flagrante* could also have acted to protect the innocent. Men inclined to honour-killing on impulse or suspicion would now have to think twice before risking a hearing in the homicide court.

One ingenious innovation was in the area of enforcement. Augustus' purpose in proscribing adultery as a 'public' offence was to prevent its occurrence, by ensuring that it would always incur punishment: 'a statutory penalty is laid down for that husband who profits in any way from the adultery and also against him who retains as his wife a woman caught in adultery' (Ulpian at D. 48.5.2.2). Husbands, therefore, who condoned adultery by their wives, could themselves be accused of *lenocinium*, acting as a pimp or procurer (McGinn 1998: 171–94). The effect of this was to extend the definition of *lenocinium*, which was already punishable by law and entailed *infamia*, loss of civil rights and of reputation. It was not required that the husband receive money or other gain for his wife's shame; the mere condoning was enough for a conviction.

As was the case with other public-law statutes, the Lex Julia on adulteries regulated the right of accusation, giving priority to husbands and fathers. If neither husband nor father acted within sixty 'competent days' (*dies utiles*), the way was open for a third party to intervene and he had four months in which to do so. The third party could be another family member, but he could also be 'qui volet', in line with the general conventions of the *publica iudicia*. If no accusation of adultery, *lenocinium* or *stuprum* was brought within five years of the alleged offence, no further legal action was possible. The statute specified the three charges only; the juristic view was that the time limit applied to all offences encompassed by the statute (D. 48.5.30(29).6–7).

Augustus' law provided for the Roman elite family what moderns describe as 'double institutionalisation' (Bohannan 1965; Lempert and Sanders 1989: 197–201 and 242–77). By this process the values expressed by one institution (e.g. monogamy by the Christian Church) are reinforced by legislation (e.g. the outlawing of bigamy), which does not replace but supplements existing institutions. The creation of a legal process of this kind requires provision for interaction between the social institution (the family) and the legal handling of the problem. Bohannan identified three types of provision: first, that the difficulties within the institution, which now threaten it, can be disengaged and then re-engaged in the legal process; second, that the legal process must be able to handle the problem; and third, the new solutions must be re-engaged within the non-legal institution from which they emerged (Bohannan 1965: 35). Augustus had answers to all three. The disengagement from family control took place through the legal process, which dictated the timing and order of events, while the threat of the accusation of *lenocinium* and the permission granted to a third party to bring an action limited the chances of a cover-up. Second, the trouble was 'handled' in a prescriptive, indeed a pre-emptive, manner, because the wife was expelled from the family by divorce prior to the hearing itself, and the child of the affair, if there was one, would follow her. Third, the wronged family would be reconstituted, its honour satisfied and its membership purified by the expulsion of the erring wife and the conviction of both the guilty.

Juristic commentary, imperial rescript and, as we shall see, the arguments of advocates modified the Augustan law in two ways. One was to clarify points left open by the wording of the original statute. The wording itself incurred the censure of Papinian (*Adulterers* 1), who observed that the law referred carelessly to *stuprum* and adultery without properly distinguishing between them (D. 48.5.6.1). A wronged father, who killed the adulterer but merely wounded his daughter, was deemed by Marcus Aurelius and Commodus to have fulfilled the condition of the statute, because his intention had been to kill both (D. 48.5.33(32)). Countering or off-setting a charge of adultery by the lodging of a counter-charge of *lenocinium* by an alleged adulterer was not permitted. A delay on the part of a husband was allowed, although the example of a summary verdict of *lenocinium* by Septimius Severus against the senator Claudius Gorgus, without an accusation having been brought, was a warning to compliant husbands (D. 48.5.2.6).

The second modification was the introduction into legal discourse of opinions that were at variance with the philosophy of the statute itself. The attempt to move family jurisdiction into the public criminal domain was deeply resented. Soon after Augustus' death (and despite his respect for that emperor's enactments) Tiberius ruled that family courts could continue to act, provided that no public accusation had been brought (Suet. *Tib.* 35.1); the effect of this would have been considerably to dilute the threat of prosecution for *lenocinium*. More important still was the jurists' respect for the emotions involved. The priority of accusation accorded to the husband over the father, probably by legal opinion rather than the statute, was justified because he would pursue the matter 'with an anger closer to his heart and greater grief' (D. 48.5.2.8). But offended honour may have been counteracted by love. Ulpian, quoting Homer to justify extension of legal control of adultery to all legal systems, wrote that 'not alone among living men do the sons of Atreus love their wives' (D. 48.5.14(13).1, citing *Iliad* 9.340). Both Agamemnon and Menelaus had suffered from adulterous wives, Clytemnestra and Helen; the latter provided a precedent for forgiveness.

The Augustan law had no time for the excuses or explanations that might have been provided by the promiscuous – or even cruel – behaviour of the husband. Ulpian (*Adulterers* 2), however, in line with the general discretion awarded in practice to judges, insisted that the presiding magistrate should investigate the behaviour of the husband. Had he 'lived modestly by himself, and set an example to his wife in the cultivation of good morals'? For, if he had not, then it was inequitable that he should ask from his wife the restraint he failed to show himself. From that it followed that the husband was culpable in bringing the charge, rather than seeking an agreement between the two of them, to allow the 'charge against one to be compensated for by the fault of the other' (D. 48.5.14(13).5). The extract does not address what might happen as a consequence of this desirable reconciliation: the husband might in turn be sued as a *leno*, for condoning his wife's fault. The fact that it does not may reflect the power of changes in social attitudes. Ulpian reflects the expectations of married couples influenced by philosophical assertions of the equal virtue of men and women, such as the Stoic Musonius Rufus and the Greek philosopher and rhetorician Plutarch, who wrote extensively on marriage, gender and the exemplary women of history.

Jurists, perhaps influenced by advocates in real cases, also asked and answered other questions which had not occurred to Augustus. A man could not accuse a wife, whom he had remarried, after there had been another husband in between, as the second marriage cancelled out the previous offence. Nor could he accuse her of *stuprum*, 'for it is too late for him to make accusations against the moral character he has approved by the act of marrying her' (D. 48.5.14(13).9–10). Jurists also ruled that rape did not constitute adultery: a woman taken prisoner might be forced to have sex (D. 48.5.14(13).7); and a woman raped may have delayed telling her husband out of shame (D. 48.5.40(39).pr.). In neither case was she liable. The cumulative effect of these interpretations was to provide some protection for women against malicious accusation and casual infidelity. That the questions were asked and were answered in the way that they were represents a greater recognition of women's rights than Augustus would have accorded. However, Septimius Severus adhered to his predecessor's ethos in one respect: women, he informed the petitioner Cassia, still could not sue for adultery, because it was forbidden by the Lex Julia (*CJ* 9.9.1).

QUINTILIAN: SCHOOL EXERCISES AND THE LAW

Largely invisible in the process of change are the arguments advanced by advocates, resulting in court decisions, which, although not formally binding as precedents, influenced the legal climate in line with social expectations. Quintilian's school-exercise cases, presented in a treatise dating from the reign of Domitian, provide a series of examples of how Augustus' law could be contested by trainee advocates. Quintilian as a 'source' for law should be used with caution (see Tellegen-Couperus 2005). Although he had practised as an advocate and he draws on his own experience when offering advice to his pupils, his cases are primarily designed for the schoolroom, where practice, as he explained, often differed from that of the courts. Some of his legal situations, such as that of the adulterous priest who was allowed to spare one life and chose his own, are clearly imaginary (5.10.104). Moreover, his examples are often drawn from the past, from Greek history and myth, from Greek forensic oratory and, most notably, from Cicero.

Quintilian's use of Roman law has not always been approved by Romanists (e.g. Robinson 2002, 2005), although a spirited defence of his contribution, and that of advocates in general, to Roman legal thought has been mounted by Crook (1995: 167–71). What is significant, however, about Quintilian's identification of legal issues as *controversiae*, matters to be argued about from opposing viewpoints (1995: 163–7), is that what is on offer is not statements of law but debating points concerning law. They identify points at which the written law may be challenged by advocates on grounds of equity or concerns of honour and other social values. What may appear to be an inaccurate statement may in fact be a deliberately incomplete suggestion, designed to provoke debate. For example, as an instance of a defence plea which admits the deed but claims that it is justified in law, Quintilian wrote, of the killing of an adulterer, 'What if he admits the deed, but declares that the adulterer was lawfully killed by him? For assuredly, there exists a law which allows this' (*Inst.* 3.6.17). Because the statement is incomplete, it appears that the killing of an adulterer was legal in all cases, which it clearly was not. But, we may suggest, there was an expectation that the budding advocates would fill the gap for themselves. This is confirmed by another case, concerning the adulterer killed in a brothel (*Inst.* 5.10.39). The statement that 'you killed the adulterer, which the law allows' is immediately qualified by mention of the place of killing. This evokes the limits placed on the act by the Lex Julia, 'but because it was in a brothel, it is homicide (*caedes*)'. This qualification of the general permission implied by the first statement supports the present contention that Quintilian's purpose was not to state what the law was but to provide the minimum information required for the conducting of the controversy by the rhetor's pupils. Thus the killing of the adulterer in the brothel was, in terms of the text of the law, homicide. However, the presence of the adulterous wife in the brothel added to the dishonourable nature of the offence and therefore the righteous anger of the offended father or husband. A second line of legal argument could also be adduced for the same situation: if a married woman took a lover while trading as a prostitute, would sleeping with her make a man liable to a charge of adultery at all (*Inst.* 7.3.6, 9–10), especially if the lover was ignorant of her marital status?

One further example, which is directly relevant to the provision in the Lex Julia that the adulterous couple must be killed at once, concerns the man (*qui*) who killed the adulterous woman, caught in the act, and later (*postea*) killed the lover in the Forum, after he had escaped (*Inst.* 3.11.7). As Olivia Robinson (2005: 65) observed, this 'would be good law for the *paterfamilias* who caught them in his own house or his son-in-law's, but in no other case'. But the defence advocate was clearly intended to have a case, which could be based on the spirit of the law as opposed to its very clear letter. He could argue, for example, that the adulterer had only just escaped or that the killer was influenced by passion and by offended honour. He might even observe that the emperor Domitian had provided a precedent when he killed his wife's lover, Paris, in the street (Dio, *Epitome* 67.3). When it is remembered that *iudices* on the standing *quaestiones* could decide what they chose, that they were all stakeholders in the 'honour' culture, and that Quintilian himself, like Cicero, paid great attention to techniques for influencing the emotions of the judge, a decision in favour of the wronged husband or father was a plausible outcome, whatever the letter of the law. This would be the line taken by at least one future emperor: a man prosecuted for homicide under the Lex Cornelia because he killed his wife caught in adultery was, in the view of Antoninus Pius (D. 48.8.1.5), entitled to leniency, although the killing was not justified under the adultery law.

The significance of Quintilian, therefore, for the law on adultery lies not in purported statements of 'what the law was' but in his illustrations of where the law might be contested. But his deliberately selective sketches of set-piece situations – the killings in the Forum or the brothel – are clearly designed with the contents of the Lex Julia in mind and they signal areas where the advocate might adduce social values to subvert the letter of the law. Reproduced in real courts, the verdicts generated by these means would, over time, change the operation of the law itself.

POENA LEGIS

The punishment for adultery stipulated by the law is uncertain, but it was probably not the death penalty. A punishment sanctioned quickly by custom was the banishment of the lovers to separate islands, but it is uncertain how far this could be applied in practice if convictions were numerous; confiscation of property and loss of civil rights were also possible penalties. A problem for the operation of the law was that elite families were likely to be reluctant to expose insults to their honour before a *quaestio* presided over by a praetor.

Private retribution or senatorial hearings were the two obvious alternative options. When Augustus' daughter, Julia, was deemed guilty of multiple adulteries, her father resorted to his traditional powers as *pater* and punished her himself with exile. The same private justice was meted out to Augustus' granddaughter, the younger Julia, exiled in AD 6. Discretion was also the policy of Tiberius towards eminent adulterers: Appuleia Varilia, who was related to Augustus, was convicted of adultery by the Senate but punished by her family with internal exile (Tac. *Ann.* 2.50). And emperors and their families continued to avenge their own wrongs. Antonia the younger, mother to Livia the younger, punished her daughter herself for her adultery and treason with Sejanus; Claudius was party to the summary execution of Messalina, who was liable for treason and perhaps for adultery as well (Tac. *Ann.* 11.29; Suet. *Claud.* 26, 29 and 36).

The Senate, as we have seen, had the power to vary punishments, and its decisions are therefore no guide to the contents of Augustus' law. The picture is further confused by the practice of accusers. Minded to exploit the flexibility of trials before the Senate, they combined adultery charges with other allegations: Aemilia Lepida was accused of adulteries, poisoning, and illegal enquiries of astrologers (Tac. *Ann.* 3.22); and Claudia Pulchra, of *stuprum* with one Furnius, poisoning and magic (*Ann.* 4.52). Some accused under Tiberius seemed to have feared a fate worse than relegation to an island. Both Aemilia Lepida, who was accused of adultery with a slave (*Ann.* 6.40), and one Albucilla, accused of multiple adulteries (*Ann.* 6.47), tried to take their own lives (Aemilia succeeded). Under Claudius, who often heard cases in private rather than in full Senate, the elder Poppaea Sabina anticipated an adultery charge from Messalina by suicide (*Ann.* 11.2).

ADULTERY IN LATE ANTIQUITY

The adultery law, as Tacitus had observed, was open to abuse by informers. However, a remedy was not offered before Constantine, who, in 326, limited the right of third-party accusation to agnate family members, these being fathers, cousins on the father's side and brothers, while retaining the priority granted to the husband (*CT* 9.7.2; Evans Grubbs 1995: 205–16). Then, probably five years later, he tightened the law on divorce by permitting unilateral divorces to a specified list of serious faults, of which adultery was one (*CT* 3.16.1). The two laws together allowed an unwilling partner to escape a marriage on grounds of adultery, only if the agnates co-operated in the process. While this might appear to impose an extra restriction, the economic inhibitions on women seeking divorce should be borne in mind. If a woman wished to leave her husband and return to her family of birth, the consent of her agnates was in practice a precondition unless the woman had substantial financial resources of her own.

In line with the austere morality of the period, Constantine associated adultery with the other 'capital' crimes of homicide and magic (*CT* 9.40.1). Throughout the fourth century it was one of a select group of heinous crimes which could not be given pardon by amnesty at Easter (*CT* 9.38.1–3; 6–8). Early in the fifth century the emperors ruled that it should have priority among cases to be heard in the governor's court (*CT* 9.2.5). There is also some evidence, referring to the 370s, that the death penalty was inflicted in some cases (Arjava 1996: 193–6). Valentinian's purge of senators in 370 netted a few adulterers (Amm. Marc. 28.1.16). A story of a saintly Christian woman, falsely accused by her husband before the governor of Aemilia Liguria in the early 370s (Jerome, *Letter* 1), assumes the existence of the death penalty for the offence (as well as torture in ascertaining the truth).

But the stern attitude adopted by the authorities towards adultery was inconsistent with the realities of human behaviour. The Christian Church took the trouble, in its Councils, to address the issue of how penitent adulterers should be treated. Early in the third century Tertullian's *De Pudicitia* took issue with the bishop of Rome over the liberal policy of his assistant, Callistus, advocating readmission of adulterers to communion. Later Church Councils accepted that adulterers, guilty of only one offence, could atone for their offences by subjecting themselves to the discipline of the Church and performing penance, perhaps remaining outside Church observances for five years (*Council of Elvira*, early fourth century, canon 69). Clearly for this to happen, the adultery had to have been admitted and the reason for the penance openly acknowledged. Such could not have been the case if the adulterers had been subjected to the full rigour of compulsory divorce, prosecution and punishment enjoined in the secular law.

CHAPTER 8

Remedies for violence

To legislate against violence was to seek to inhibit forms of behaviour endemic to Roman culture. Self-help through direct physical and frequently violent action was both socially and legally recognised (Nippel 1995: 35–9). The Roman state was founded on the fratricide of Remus by Romulus, the successful 'founder', who added to his achievement the perpetuation of his city's population through the rape of the Sabine women. Roman military conquest was accompanied by mass murder, brazenly publicised: Caesar boasted of having killed over a million Gauls (Pliny, *Natural History* 7.92). The suffering of the vanquished was displayed on public monuments, paralleling the agonies of criminals in the amphitheatre, where painful and protracted death became entertainment, reassuring Romans of their own place in the world (M. Zimmerman 2006: 347; Coleman 1990, 1998). Physical violence and, with it, violent self-help were an institutionalised part of Roman society.

Early civil procedures made it the responsibility of the plaintiff to produce the defendant in court, by physical means such as grasping him by the hand (*manus iniectio*) if necessary (*RS* II, 584–90). As we have seen, the law recognised the right of the citizen to kill in certain situations, in defence of property or honour. The thief who came by night could be killed by the householder in self-defence; the offender against family honour could be subjected to the summary justice of the *paterfamilias* and the family council. The jurisdiction of the family also extended into the public sphere. The Roman historians proudly recorded the executions of several traitors by their fathers or family councils as late as 63 BC (Oros. 4.13.18; Dio 37.36.4), although some fathers who overreacted to filial misconduct could find themselves prosecuted for murder and punished by the state (Cic. *Balb.* 28).

Violence and its consequences generated both civil and public procedures. The requirement that property should be protected, not only from burglars but also from gangs, involved the praetor's policing powers, through a set of interdicts on violent dispossession. Intimidation, or creation of fear (*metus*), permitted restitution under the Edict; its text initially specified both force and fear, only to abandon the former as redundant (D. 4.2.1). The fear must be real, not the apprehensions experienced by the timorous (D. 4.2.5–6), and the danger immediate. Acknowledging by implication the Roman authorities' dependence on healthy terror, Ulpian exempts the fear caused by magistrates in the exercise of their duties, provided that they acted within the law (D. 4.2.3).

Civil remedies for damage to persons and property could also be sought through the Lex Aquilia on damages (see chapter 2), which also covered the killing of slaves, and the laws on outrage (*iniuria*). Homicide and some other violent acts, such as arson, were proscribed by Sulla's Lex Cornelia on assassins and poisoners (*de sicariis et veneficis*); the punishment for the low-status urban arsonist under the Empire was, appropriately, to be burned alive. Confusion between homicide and violence was easy and natural. Sulla's homicide law stated that people who carried weapons could be liable but that self-protection was a legitimate defence, an opinion reiterated in Paulus' *Sententiae*; however, the compilers of the Digest (D. 48.6.11.2) included Paulus' opinion in its section on *vis*. Sulla's law had also made liable those who carried weapons with the intent to kill, even if they were not in the end used.

In Sulla's day a number of violent actions threatening the security of the community were not covered by statute. When one of the consuls of 78, Lepidus, joined a revolt, the other consul, Q. Lutatius Catulus, passed the first law on public violence (*vis*); a second, the Lex Plautia *de vi*, was passed between 78 and 63, when a threat of its use was invoked against Catiline. The Lex Lutatia (Robinson 1995: 78–80) outlawed armed attacks on magistrates, the seizure of public places and, perhaps, bearing arms against the public interest. It may also have removed the right to own by possession property seized in the course of sedition, and the enlisting of gangs to cause public disturbances. The initial purpose was to protect public order from troublesome outsiders.

Both Caesar and Augustus showed their concern for public order by passing laws of their own on *vis*, which built on the Lex Lutatia (Cloud 1988, 1989); it is known that the penalty under Caesar's law was interdiction from fire and water (Cic. *Phil.* 1.21–3). With Augustus came a change of emphasis: the abuse of office by magistrates through killing, flogging and otherwise maltreating Roman citizens was added, thus assimilating the law to others ensuring the accountability of the governors to the governed. In, probably, the second century unlawful violence on the part of magistrates and officials became known as *vis publica* and was distinguished from *vis privata*, which, though still a public crime, carried a lesser penalty.

VIOLENCE AND THE CROWD

It was, for obvious reasons, not possible to prosecute a mob for rioting; crowd control was a policing matter (Nippel 1995: 47–69). A crowd of thousands could not be sued (although selected individuals could be, and were, brought to trial). But the Roman authorities' relative tolerance of riots was not motivated only by their tacit acknowledgement of the incapacity of their policing authorities to deal with them. Mass demonstrations, some of which became riots, were a recognised means of communication between the governing elites and the mass of the population. The early Republican constitution had been shaped by a series of secessions of the plebs in defence of their rights and freedom (*libertas*). In the first century BC Republican politicians constructed the support shown in public meetings (*contiones*) for their policies as validation of their status as representatives of the notionally sovereign *populus* (Mouritsen 2001: 38–62); for example, Cicero in April 43 (*Phil.* 14.5.12–14) and Augustus in 22 (*Res Gestae* 5.1) both made a virtue of 'refusing' the dictatorship when offered by the crowd. In the 50s Clodius (tribune in 58) and his opponents allowed such crowd demonstrations to develop into more violent and systematic assertions of mob control of the streets (Tatum 1996). Mobs were (within limits) an essential part of the functioning of Republican competitive politics (Millar 1998).

It was also accepted that a crowd might resort to violent demonstrations in its collective interest when the government failed to honour its obligations. Both at Rome and in some cities elsewhere the food supply was the responsibility of the ruling city council. When the supplies failed, the crowd made its views known. The consuls of 75 and 74 BC were pelted with stones at Rome; in Prusa, *c.* 100 AD, a mob menaced the house of Dio Chrysostom, blaming him for a food shortage, and was only turned back by the narrowness of the approach road (Dio Chrys. *Discourse* 46.12). In his speech to the crowd defending his actions he reminded them that riots were a policing matter for the Roman authorities, threatening retaliation by the proconsul (46.14). In Late Antiquity there were still more pressing reasons to conciliate crowds: their acclamations or shouts of abuse were reported to the emperor as evidence of the popularity or otherwise of governors (*CT* 1.16.6.1); and emperors themselves, when they visited Rome, respected and even responded to the freedom of speech that was the ancestral right of the Roman People (Lactant. *De mort. pers.* 17.2 of Diocletian; Amm. Marc. 16.10.3 of Constantius II).

But relations between the mobs and their rulers were not always so harmonious. Caligula encapsulated the problem that autocrats confronted when dealing with crowds – their lack of a single neck, which could be hacked through (Suet. *Calig.* 30). Commodus was forced to sacrifice his favourite minister Cleander to mass demonstrations in 190; his suspicion that the latter was orchestrated from behind the scenes by dissident senators, who ceded control of the streets to the rioters, led to a purge of his opponents once order had been restored (Dio, *Epitome* 73.13). In the mid fourth century the Elder Symmachus' house in the Transtiberine area of Rome was burned down, after a rumour was spread by a 'cheap plebeian' that he had refused to issue cheap wine to the populace, as he would rather use it to quench his limekilns (Amm. Marc. 27.3.4); the house of his successor as Prefect of the City, Lampadius, was also attacked by the mob, who failed to damage it and were driven off by Lampadius' friends and neighbours (Amm. Marc. 27.3.8). In 410, when Rome was under attack by the Goths under Alaric, the Prefect of Rome, Gabinius Pompeianus, was lynched by the mob, who blamed him for the food shortage caused by the siege; Christians ascribed blame for the Prefect's violent end to his pagan convictions (*Life of Melania* 19 (Greek), 2.1 (Latin); Zosimus, *New History* 5.41.1). Nor were the crowd always immune from retaliation by the authorities. When, in 387, an Antiochene crowd rioted against the emperor Theodosius I and toppled his statues, the whole population found itself at risk from an emperor who was not afraid to kill *en masse*: only pleas for mercy and interventions by the local Christian leadership deflected the wrath of the angry emperor (Browning 1952; Stewart 1999).

Control of crowd violence was, therefore, a policing matter. Its operation was restricted by the conventions, which allowed free demonstrations of opinion, and by the limits on the resources available to the authorities. But, if individual rioters could hope for safety in numbers, those who fomented disturbances could find themselves liable, as promoters of seditions and riots, who could incur punishment under the laws on public violence and perhaps treason as well. In Late Antiquity those who incited seditions and riots could expect to be crucified, thrown to the wild beasts or deported (Paulus, *Sent.* 5.22). However, a situation could be best defused by exposing the pretensions of the leading agitators; in 356, during a wine shortage at Rome, one Petrus Valvomeres was recognised by the Prefect, publicly humiliated before 'his' crowd and then released, to show the authorities' contempt for his behaviour (Amm. Marc. 15.7.4; Matthews 1989: 417–18).

In Late Antiquity the priorities of justice could be distorted by local factors and imperial policies, particularly on religion. Laws in the Theodosian Code proscribed attacks on Christians by pagans (*CT* 16.4.3, of 392) and by Christians on other peaceful citizens (*CT* 16.10.4, of 423); this was in line with traditional imperial dislike of public disorder. But justice was selective. In the 380s the pagan Libanius tried, without success, to persuade Theodosius I to rein in his over-zealous official Maternus Cynegius, by complaining, in his oration *On the Temples*, of Christian attacks and religious riots. In 408, in North Africa, a pagan crowd attacked and stoned the local Christian church at Calama, the base for Augustine's friend and later biographer, Possidius. The local authorities refused to act, the clergy found themselves isolated and an appeal was made to the emperor, who ordered stern measures against the rioters, perhaps including apprehension of the leaders of the riot and the use of the local militia if the civil power was unable (or unwilling) to act (*Const. Sirmondianae* 14, possibly a later forgery; Aug. *Letters* 90–1, 97, 104; Harries 1998: 88–91). The Christian bias of the sources obscures aspects of this last affair less favourable to their case; their isolation suggests lack of local support and the intrusion into local politics of a vengeful imperial constitution was unlikely to help the Christian cause over the longer term.

THE LEX JULIA *DE VI* AND ITS COMMENTATORS

Violence, as we have seen, was not only an offence in its own right under public criminal law, but also an attribute of other crimes and offences punishable under the laws of delict. Constantine, with characteristic use of non-technical language, admitted that there were numerous problems with defining and acting on violence (*CT* 9.10.1). 'Many bad actions (*facinora*)', he (or his draftsman) wrote, 'are included under the one label of violence (*violentia*).' He also acknowledged that violence begets violence and that it may be hard to know who started it: 'beatings (*verbera*) and murders (*caedes*) are often found to have been perpetrated when some attempt violence and others angrily resist them'. The law on violence therefore had problems peculiar to itself: its remit was flexible; convictions would be complicated if both parties had engaged in violent behaviour; and, behind these complications, was the further consideration that Romans had the right to use violence in self-defence – a right conceded, wrote Paulus, by the laws of nations.

The noun *vis* has no genitive (or dative) case and there could therefore be no *crimen* of *vis*; the action would be brought under the statute *de vi*, and the commentators on the Lex Julia discussed the law in those terms. Without the text of the original statute, it is hard to distinguish between its original contents and offences which may have been assimilated later. The overlap with other public criminal statutes and with civil procedures was inevitably extensive, resulting over time in recognition that victims of 'violence' had an exceptionally wide choice of remedies available to them, both criminal and civil. The Lex Julia encompassed violent actions both by individuals (labelled by later jurists *vis privata*) and also by those magistrates and others who abused their *imperium*. Actions by individuals included mob attacks on villas and armed seizure of property (including property from burning buildings and fires, D. 48.6.3.5); armed expulsion of a possessor (owner-occupier) of a house, farm or ship (D. 48.6.3.6); rape (*stuprum per vim*) of a boy, woman or any other (D. 48.6.3.4), and forcible abduction of a freeborn boy (D. 48.6.6); arson backed by mob violence (D. 48.6.5.pr, clearly also covered by the Lex Cornelia); wrongful imprisonment; and interference with burials and funerals (D. 48.6.5.pr.). In line with the principles of other public criminal statutes, evidence of conspiracy and intent was sufficient to justify a charge. The statute caught those who gathered a crowd together and incited a riot (but not the crowd itself); and those who kept an armed household (*familia*) of slaves and/ or freedmen and carried weapons themselves. It also extended to those who collected weapons beyond what was necessary for hunting or self-protection on journeys (as these could clearly be used to equip small private armies); however, inherited collections were exempt (D. 48.6.1–2). Accusations could also be brought if holders of *imperium* used unlawful violence on Roman citizens, or if the judicial process was frustrated by violence or *iniuria* (D. 48.6.10.pr.).

The supply of helpful lists supplementing the original legislation could not disguise the basic difficulties of legislating on criminal violence in the first place. As we have seen, many forms of harm inflicted by individuals on each other could be remedied by either civil or criminal proceedings. Problems of definition, its status as an attribute of other actions, some criminal some not, and questions of what started or provoked the violence in the first place made the law of violence an exceptionally flexible instrument of retaliation. By 378 it was a source of pride to the imperial quaestor that the lucky litigant had a choice of civil or criminal remedies in very many areas, including the suppression of wills, the status of freedmen, theft and kidnapping and – the example round which the constitution is based – the action for violent dispossession (*CT* 9.20.1): by a 'majority of jurists', wrote Gratian's legal draftsman, it had been agreed that where a civil and criminal action were both available, both could be brought, thus a person dispossessed by violence could employ the praetorian interdict *unde vi* to recover possession but could also bring an accusation under the Lex Julia *de vi*. This was presented as a great favour to litigants; others might think that the main beneficiaries would be the lawyers.

CIVIL REMEDIES

Under the Roman Republic the praetor, and especially the *praetor urbanus*, had charge of civil disputes between citizens (the *praetor peregrinus* handled disputes of Romans with non-citizens). The praetor had extensive policing powers; his *imperium*, the right to issue military commands, was no matter of form. He had the power to grant actions to anyone who wished to sue for robbery with violence. The robber was also liable for violence at one remove if he could be shown to have assembled his gang with premeditated bad intent. The penalties were analogous to those governing theft: one who seized goods by violence was liable for both non-manifest theft (double the value) and the quadruple penalty for taking goods by force (D. 47.8.1).

Armed-gang violence might also cause loss or damage to the victim but not result in the theft of anything. This gap in the provisions of the Edict was plugged by the further offence of *tumultus*, public disturbance or riot. However, as noted above, bringing an action against a mob was not viable. Instead, the Edict dealt with material loss which took place in the course of a *tumultus* and which was inflicted deliberately. But for an action to be brought, a *tumultus* had also to be defined. Two men – or even three or four – engaged in a brawl (*rixa*) were too few to count as a riot, but ten to fifteen men were sufficient to create a mob (D. 47.8.4.3). The burden of proof on the plaintiff was relatively modest: he did not have to establish that the defendant had summoned the crowd, merely that he did so with the intention of causing damage.

Much of the praetor's work concerned disputes over property and possession, and included allegations about unlawful, or violent, dispossession, to which he usually responded by issuing his interdict, *unde vi*, which ordered the new possessor to vacate the property until the issues of ownership were resolved. It did not make a judgement on who in fact owned the property, but failure to observe the order to leave would result in further action. In the late 70s or early 60s BC this was supplemented with the interdicts on ejection 'by force', or 'by armed force' (*vi armata*), which formed the subject of part of the lawsuits between Aulus Caecina, who was defended by Cicero, and Aebutius, his rival for a disputed inheritance (Frier 1985).

The interdict *unde vi* read (D. 43.16.1.1):

Where by force you or your staff of slaves (*familia*) have ejected such a one, I will grant a judgement about that place within a year with respect to what he had there then, and after a year with respect to what has come into the hands of that person who forcibly ejected him.

For the interdict to be invoked, the fact of previous possession had to be established (which was one of Caecina's difficulties); in the absence of documents such as title deeds, this could be done by calling neighbours or local city councillors as witnesses, or citation of the tax records of the claimant. The right of action was also allowed to landowners whose tenants had been forced out (D. 43.16.20).

The interdict *de vi* (*armata*) was a response to a graver offence than that of mere eviction; it implied that force and intimidation were also used. The initiator of the violence was liable to a civil penalty if found guilty and so had to be clearly identified. Many jurists, including Sabinus (D. 43.16.1.11), Cassius (1.27), Proculus (1.25), Antistius Labeo (1.29), and Salvius Julianus (1.31, 35) as well as Ulpian's commentary on the Edict, offered opinions on who could be held responsible for ejection. These included not only those who were physically involved, but also those who gave the orders (D. 43.16.1.12). A municipality could be on the receiving end of an interdict (D. 43.16.4, Pomponius), and ejection could be held to have taken place even though the owner might not have been present in person, as in the case of summer and winter pastures, which would be unoccupied for part of the year (D. 43.16.1.25), or because the possessor was absent on a journey (D. 43.16.1.24). What constituted the 'armed' element of the force used had also to be defined; the category of 'weapon' included not only swords, spears and lances, but also sticks and stones, whether brought by the attackers or picked up on the spot. Even if they were not used, the threat of arms also constituted armed violence (D. 43.16.3.2). Again, self-defence justified the use of armed force by the possessor; in line with legal principle, he had also to establish before the judge that the attackers were indeed armed and that the acts of resistance took place at the time of the assault and not later (D. 43.16.3.9).

The interdict was intended as a helpful measure, to enable restoration of the previous state of things, while the legal issues were properly sorted out. In fact, it further complicated matters, by creating two suits in place of one. Once the public laws on violence were also invoked, further potential for delay and confusion was created, because the petitioner for the interdict on grounds of violence could also resort to a public, criminal accusation against his adversary (see further, Harries 2006b). Emperors may even have contradicted each other about which case, the ownership suit or the public or private action for violence, should be heard first. Septimius Severus and Caracalla upheld an appeal from one Marcus Priscus on the grounds that the *iudex* should have heard the question of right of possession before the suit on forcible dispossession (*CJ* 7.62.1, of 209; Peachin 1996: 52–3). This reversed the ruling of Antoninus Pius, writing to the Thessalians, that the case of violence should be tried first (D. 48.6.5.1, Marcian). Pius' preferred order was to be followed by Constantine, who had the bright idea of making the penalty inflicted on the person found guilty on the first charge (that of violence) dependent on the outcome of the second (*CT* 9.10.3). If a litigant lost both (i.e. he was both violent and not the rightful owner), he was liable to deportation and confiscation of all his goods; in other words, although both suits may have been matters of civil law, he would face a criminal penalty. Alternatively, if the man guilty of violence in the first suit was found to be the rightful owner, the penalty was limited to confiscation of half the disputed property. All this assumed, of course, that both suits ran their course and were completed and that the man found guilty on the first charge did not absent himself rather than face the consequences of losing the second. Although Constantine's ingenious innovation was included in the Theodosian Code, which validates it as law, in 506 the Gallo-Roman compilers of the *Breviarium* of Alaric deleted it as unworkable.

But why should a litigant brave the displeasure of the authorities by pre-empting the judicial process? A creditor who seized possession of an estate in payment of a debt, without use of physical force, might understandably have assumed that he had merely asserted his rights. Such was not the view of Marcus Aurelius, who held that if a creditor, Marcian (not the jurist), had seized possession before the law had run its course, he was guilty of *vis* and had thus forfeited his claim. The exchange between them was pre-served in court records available to the provincial jurist Callistratus (*On Legal Hearings*, 5) and included twice in the Digest, first in the section on the praetorian remedy for intimidation (*metus*, D. 4.2.13) and secondly under the Lex Julia *de vi* (D. 48.7.7):

(MARCUS)   It is best that, if you think you have claims, you should pursue them by actions at law; meanwhile the other party should remain in possession – you are the claimant.

(MARCIAN)   I have not committed *vis*.

(MARCUS)   Do you think *vis* occurs only when men suffer physical injuries? It occurs when anyone demands what he thinks is owed to him otherwise than through the agency of a judge. I really do not think it consistent with your self-respect (*verecundia*), status (*dignitas*) or sense of right (*pietas*) to do something unlawful. Whoever then shall be proved to me to have taken possession unilaterally and without resort to a judge of any property of a debtor, which had not been (formally) handed over to him by the debtor, and to have said that he has a right over that property, shall not have creditor's rights.

As far as the exchange goes, the point at issue, on which Marcus Aurelius adjudicated, was the illegality of making any claim, including one by force, on a disputed estate without the authority of a judge. He states no opinion on whether Marcian has in fact seized possession unlawfully. However, the judgement does extend the meaning of *vis* to encompass any unlawful seizure of property, whether or not physical violence was used.

The use of Marcus' judgement under two separate headings by the compilers of the Digest reflects changes in the legal culture of violence in general. The context of Marcus' judgement is clearly civil; if Marcian is shown to have acted unlawfully, he will forfeit his debt. But although Marcian's case is a civil one, the Digest compilers also included it in their discussion of the Lex Julia, in effect criminalising it by its inclusion in the 'public law' context. In fact, under the Lex Julia *de vi*, Marcian, if found guilty, would have faced confiscation of one-third of his goods and loss of status: he would also be debarred from becoming a senator, decurion or holder of any government post and would be treated as if *infamis* (D. 48.7.1 and 8) – penalties that were clearly inapplicable in his case.

The Digest's handling of the Marcian case illustrates its broader tendency to impose on past legal interpretation of the public criminal law the assumptions of its own day. Its publication in 533 was over four hundred years after the date ascribed to Salvius Julianus' codification of the Praetor's Edict, in 130. Since that time, the Edict had been interpreted by extensive juristic commentaries (which responded to the legal climates of the second and third centuries) and by successive imperial rulings, which were issued in response to situations as they arose and reflected the emperor's and his advisers' understanding of law at the time. Despite this, the compilers of the Digest were guided by the Commentaries on the Edict by Ulpian and others, in their treatment of unlawful ejection from possession in general, and analysed the interdict *unde vi* in Book 43.16 as part of the praetor's law; the Theodosian Code had also treated the interdict in its 'edictal' Book 4. However, when the Digest compilers considered robbery with violence and damage inflicted through *tumultus*, they ignored the praetor's role. Instead, they assimilated both to theft and the law of delicts in general, and they placed both in Book 47. In terms of the operation of the law in their own day, this was fair comment. But it is also a warning as to how the legal tradition may experience even inadvertent reinvention, thus obscuring or distorting the historical facts of its evolution.

CONCLUSION

The law on violence originated from a time of crisis; faced with armed revolt on the part of his fellow-consul, Lutatius Catulus legislated to limit public disorder. His targets were not the mobs but those who planned and fomented violence and sedition, especially in the City. While the planners of riots were not necessarily members of the elite, they were people who had an interest in causing trouble; the agents of Clodius and his opponents in the 50s were implicated in the organisation of disorder but were not prominent players in the political game. Petrus Valvomeres in 356, with his distinctive red hair, was an agitator well known to the authorities; later exiled, he was involved in a sex scandal and came to a bad end (Amm. Marc. 15.7.5). Some forms of violence were clearly available to any individual who saw fit, say, to indulge in rape, or interference with a burial or funeral. But the Lutatian law and its successors also envisaged *vis* as an elite crime. Augustus gave it a specifically public dimension by including violence on the part of magistrates, but gang violence in general implies someone behind it.

When victims of violence in the countryside sought redress, the outcomes were unpredictable. The law had in its sights the 'Mr Bigs' who expelled the humbler owners of desirable properties by force; or who ran their households as if they were a private army and interned their victims in private prisons, an offence which, in Late Antiquity, was assimilated to treason (*CT* 9.11; cf. Robinson 1968). Violence was a crime of the powerful, inflicted on the powerless, whose powers of achieving justice were limited by the operation of patronage and the continuing tendency of the elite to look after its own. When, in 384, one Scirtius of Praeneste (Symm. *Relatio* 28; Vera 1981: 202–20; Harries 2006b) petitioned the Prefect of the City, Symmachus, for reinstatement in a disputed property, it quickly emerged that he had been forcibly expelled by the agents of the prominent (and Christian) senator Q. Clodius Hermogenianus Olybrius. Worse, the agent had imprisoned in a villa the entire town council of Praeneste, so that they could not bear witness about Scirtius' occupancy of the estate. If law mirrored life, Scirtius' claim for violence would be undisputed. But Scirtius was up against the powerful, and there were problems with the documentation; although he had the sympathy of his judge, the whole business was postponed until the emperor could take cognisance of it himself.

Self-help was condoned, to a point, as a means of settling disputes between individuals, which avoided the trouble of taking matters to court. Crowd violence was a part of how rulers and ruled communicated with each other. Many powerful people operated beyond, or above, the reach of the law and even honest judges were obliged by fear or class loyalty to turn a blind eye to abuse or deflect the responsibility to supply a remedy elsewhere. For all these reasons, the good intentions of legislators were frustrated, to the point when violence could even be taken for granted. Varro's dialogue on matters agricultural was set in the Temple of Tellus, from which the attendant was unexpectedly absent. His reaction to the news of the attendant's murder may be read as representative: 'we all departed, more in sorrow at human misfortune than surprise that such a crime should have been perpetrated at Rome' (*De re rustica* 1.69.4).

CHAPTER 9

Representations of murder

Killing people was not always wrong. Enemies were killed lawfully in war; the outlaw could be killed out of hand, as could the adulterer and the thief, provided certain conditions were met. Killing in self-defence was an accepted and universal justification, although the killer might have to run the risk of proving his case in a court of law. As the political gangster T. Annius Milo found in 52, the plea that he killed his political rival Clodius in self-defence, entered on his behalf by Cicero and published as the *Pro Milone*, failed to prevent his exile. Other Cicero speeches in defence of alleged murderers took a different line. Both Sextus Roscius of Ameria, accused of parricide in 80, and, in 66, Aulus Cluentius Habitus, who was alleged to have killed his stepfather several years earlier, were defended by a combination of outright denial and vilification of the motives of the prosecution team (and, in the Cluentius case, of the victim as well). Cicero's technique was to combine a discussion of the facts with allegations about character and he had little to say on points of law.

Murder was, then as now, both serious and fascinating. Unexpected or unexplained deaths required explanation. Famous, convenient or mysterious deaths generated conspiracy theories. In the absence of forensic or medical evidence, death by poison was more easily alleged than proved – or disproved. Poison was widely suspected as the cause of the death of Germanicus in AD 19, but at the trial of Piso on various charges before the Senate the following year the charge failed to stick. Writers in the second and third centuries AD noted the number of convenient deaths which left the way open for the accession of Tiberius in AD 14: clearly (they thought) this must have been due to the murderous machinations of his mother, Livia.

THE LEX CORNELIA AND THE SC SILANIANUM

The crime of homicide was codified in Sulla's law in 80 BC (*RS* II, 749–54; Cloud 1968, 1969). Apart from refinements of definition, forensic arguments about the Lex Cornelia *de sicariis* in general came down to a question of 'whodunit' (Riggsby 1999: 78). Sulla's law, which survived Caesar's and Augustus' reforms of other courts intact, covered open and covert murder (see Cic. *Clu.* 148; *Cael.* 51) and quickly became the governing statute for all forms of homicide. It also came to include arson (Cic. *Paradoxa Stoicorum* 31) and actions in general which caused death, and it extended to judicial malpractice resulting in condemnations in the criminal courts (Cic. *Clu.* 144–57). The law also emphasised intention. If a man carried arms, intending to kill, that was equivalent to the deed itself (Cic. *Rab. Perd.* 19; *Mil.* 11). Although courts for assassins and poisoners may have existed before, Sulla's was the first attempt since the Twelve Tables (Ferrary 1991: 434) to systematise the process by which the community could punish the taking of life (see also Cloud 1968, 1969). The person who could expect punishment was the person who caused the death, directly or indirectly. Rhetorical school exercises, which also shaped legal discourse, played with ideas of indirect causation: one dispute, for example, concerned a man who had sexually abused a freeborn boy; the boy then committed suicide because of the rape. The argument for the defence was that the man was liable for a fine, for the rape, but not for homicide, as he was not the 'cause of death' (Quint. *Inst.* 4.2.68; 7.4.42).

Senatorial and imperial decisions clarified the application of the statute. A senatorial resolution clarified that a bad example was to count as equivalent to a bad intent (D. 48.8.3). The Senate also extended the list of offences covered by the *poena* of the law to include causing a riot, conniving through false witness at the conviction of the innocent, and castration (D. 48.8.4; 6; 11). In Late Antiquity two Diocletianic rulings (*CJ* 9.16.5(6) and 6(7), of 294) refer to liability 'under the Lex Cornelia'; the second reaffirms the principle, known to have been present in the statute, that carrying a weapon with intent counted as the equivalent of the deed. The Justinianic compilers added other rescripts to their section '*ad legem Corneliam*' which were not connected to the law by their authors. One, from Caracalla, reassures a soldier that he is not liable for homicide if he killed one Iustus by accident (*CJ* 9.16.1, of 215), a principle reiterated by Diocletian (*CJ* 9.16.4(5)). Both 'Theodosius' and 'Justinian' proscribed infanticide as equivalent to homicide (*CT* 9.14.1 = *CJ* 9.16.7, of 372).

One controversial consequence of murder within the household was that those slaves who were under the same roof and failed to come to the assistance of their master were made subject to a 'public investigation' and then collectively to the death penalty by the SC Silanianum. Characteristically, the jurists dissected the vocabulary of the *senatusconsultum*, defining in turn 'master' (D. 29.5.1.1; 6–11), 'slave' (29.5.1.2–5) and 'killed' (29.5.1 17–20), the point of the last being that the violence exerted had to be overt and therefore preventable; poisoning could not be prevented, unless administered by violence (29.5.1.19). Slaves would be exempted from their obligation to protect their masters if they were locked up and unable to get out, too old to help, deaf, blind, dumb (provided shouting was the only recourse) or mad (D. 29.5.3.7–11). As a rule, those too young to help were also exempt. However, in an example of a court ruling providing legal precedent, the legate Trebius Germanus executed a slave boy, who was just short of puberty, on the grounds that as he slept in his master's room and was of an age to understand he should have intervened (D. 29.5.14, see above p. 8).

The resolution was activated and vigorously challenged in a notorious case in the reign of Nero. The Prefect of the City of Rome, Pedanius Secundus, was murdered by one of his slaves because of a private dispute over manumission or a rivalry in love. All the slaves living 'under the same roof' were condemned, but a vocal minority in the Senate, supported by a noisy street demonstration, protested against the harshness of the sentence. As Tacitus (who had access to senatorial minutes) reported, this provoked a justification of the law from the distinguished consular jurist C. Cassius Longinus (Tac. *Ann.* 14. 43–4). Cassius' justification was based on fear. Masters were afraid of their slaves and always had been, although the risks were greater now that slaves were drawn from many lands and cultures. It was likely, Cassius said, that the murderer had let slip some words, or someone had noticed that he had acquired a weapon, or had seen him making his way through the house with his light; the other slaves had a duty to disclose what they knew and needed to be controlled through fear of the consequences to them of failure. While Cassius conceded that the execution of innocent people was unjust, the fate of a few individuals was justified as contributing to the public good (*utilitas publica*) as a whole.

Cassius did not have things all his own way. Early in the second century Pliny manipulated senatorial procedures to prevent a vote that would have condemned slaves and freedmen of a master found dead (Letter 8.14). Among lawyers, however, Tacitus' (or Cassius') language was echoed by Ulpian. The justification for the SC Silanianum was the consideration of public safety and the avoidance of uncertainty that underlay the concept of 'public' offences. 'No one can be safe', he wrote, 'if slaves are not compelled to guard their masters' (D. 29.5.1.pr). But because the measure was one concerning the interrogation under torture and executions of slaves, not free citizens, the jurists discussed the matter not under the Lex Cornelia but in connection with the Praetor's Edict and, in Justinian's Digest, the proper time for the opening of wills (which could be delayed by the murder investigation).

The slaves may also have been the killers themselves and, if so, became liable under the Lex Cornelia. Pliny's *Letters* record a case of the killing by his own slaves of a master notorious for his harsh treatment of them. The compilers of the Digest also acknowledged the connection of the SC Silanianum with the Lex Cornelia: Gaius' commentary on the Provincial Edict stipulated the rewards for accusers who hunted down and convicted guilty slaves – even if they had been freed by the will of the owner (D. 29.5.3.25.pr.); anyone who harboured a murderous slave was also liable under Sulla's law (29.5.3.12).

APULEIUS, PROCESS AND PARODY

Murder took many forms. The *venena* explicitly outlawed by Sulla could refer to 'drugs' as well as poison (although more often the latter) and drugs included potions and other charms. There was therefore an implicit connection between murder and magic. The North African rhetor Apuleius was an expert in this area in at least two respects. In *c.* 159 he was put on trial for his life before the governor, accused of criminal magic; his *Apology*, or *Pro Magia*, is his speech in his own defence on that occasion, although the published version may benefit from extensive rhetorical embellishments introduced after the event. Secondly, he wrote a novel, the *Metamorphoses* or *Golden Ass*, based on a Greek original, about a man who was turned into a donkey by magic. Although set in a magical Thessaly and full of witches and unlikely marvels, much of what Apuleius describes can be paralleled elsewhere (Millar 1981). Some incidents have a strong element of parody, which would be lost if the procedures satirised were not instantly recognisable. The 'interrogation', for example, of a witness consisting of a corpse brought back to life by necromancy to testify to the innocence of his wife, who was accused of his murder (*Met.* 2.27), depends for its effect on the reader's appreciation of the public cross-questioning of witnesses in criminal trials.

Apuleius knew his Roman law and makes frequent reference to the public-law statutes (Summers 1970: 513–15), including the Lex Julia on adulteries (*Met.* 6.22) and the 'penalty of the sack' for parricide (*Met.* 10.6). In the *Apology* also he observes, ironically, that the Lex Julia on marriages among the orders does not specify where a marriage should take place (*Apol.* 88.3); the appointment of a guardian for a fatherless child is mentioned (68.6); the procedures for reporting births are mentioned (89.2), as also the designation of a guardian for a woman (101.6). But this parade of knowledge would be pointless if his hearers and readers were not similarly aware of Roman law and legal process.

The humour of the *Metamorphoses* depends on Apuleius' audience's awareness of how the Roman legal system worked. Lucius, not yet a donkey, is brought to trial for a triple murder by a community which is celebrating a Festival of Laughter (*Met.* 3.2–9); the 'dead bodies' are in fact wineskins attacked by Lucius when he was drunk. The trial has 'Greek' (Colin 1965) and 'Roman' elements. Lucius is indicted by the local magistrate (not the governor), arrested by two lictors and publicly escorted to the tribunal in the Forum. At the crowd's insistence, the show is moved to the Theatre. In line with public-court procedure, the accuser, the Prefect of the Night Watch, is called on by name, and the speeches of the advocates on both sides are regulated by a water clock. The prosecution case depends on the eye-witness testimony of the Prefect, while Lucius' case adduces the plea of self-defence, which is consistent with the Lex Cornelia but also universal. In addition, Lucius claims to be of good character although, as a stranger, his claim is unsupported.

The account has a dream-like quality, the product of Lucius' inebriated condition. Like the rules and terminology of the statute itself, the context is Roman: the crowd, who will give the verdict, is addressed by both sides as '*Quirites*', Roman citizens, and Lucius is an 'alien' (*peregrinus*). In the 'dream' every worst option feared by a defendant becomes a reality. The relatives of the deceased press for a penalty to 'fit the crime', and the judge suspects the existence of accomplices and orders torture of the suspect, Greek-style. Whether he is a citizen or not, Lucius is of respectable status, yet his rights are ignored by the local court and crowd and he faces crucifixion, the fate not merely of the lower orders but of slaves (see Aubert 2002). Only when Lucius is instructed to view the bodies (i.e. the wineskins) is the joke revealed and recompense offered.

Despite the humour, there was a serious point behind the laughter. For Lucius, this is a joke which goes too far, and he refuses to accept the offers of the locals to make good the injury done to him. Moreover, the world of the *Metamorphoses* is not one where justice always prevails. Land is unlawfully seized by a powerful individual from rightful owners, who fail to get redress (*Met.* 9.35–6); a soldier grabs property that is not his (namely Lucius as a donkey) from a humble gardener, who is then falsely accused of theft by the soldier's comrades, arrested, tried and summarily executed (*Met.* 9.39–42). And the stranger was always vulnerable, lacking as he did the local network, which might provide protection; one such is accused by shepherds of theft (of Lucius) and murder of a boy, tried and punished (*Met.* 7.26).

Apuleius knew from experience what it was like to be a stranger on trial for his life. In *c.* 159 AD he was brought to a real trial before the proconsul C. Claudius Maximus at his assizes at Sabratha (in modern Libya) in a scenic location overlooking the Mediterranean (Bradley 1997). The case was a family feud conducted by legal means. The nominal accuser, Sicinius Pudens, was a member of a prominent family in the neighbouring town of Oea and the only surviving son of his widowed mother, Pudentilla, now the wife of the defendant. As he was still a minor, the case was conducted by his adult relations although, as they were not the formal accusers, they would escape liability if the charge failed (*Apol.* 2.3).

As we have it, Apuleius' speech in his own defence is a showpiece, ornate in style and adorned with learned quotations from Greek philosophers and others, a public performance characteristic of the Second Sophistic. Although this could represent Apuleius' actual strategy, at least in outline, the fact that the case was heard before a single judge should prompt caution. Apuleius' theatricals are therefore somewhat out of line with developing court practice, not only in terms of style but also because no space is allowed for interventions on the part of the judge. On the other hand, this was no typical case, but one which would have attracted wide interest. The speech shows the governor and his *consilium* (*Apol.* 1.1; 65.8; 67.5; 99.1), sitting high on their tribunal (85.2; 99.1), and a crowd of supporters; by adopting crowd-pleasing devices, Apuleius may have hoped to sway the judge in his favour.

It is assumed, on the basis of the form of indictment supplied by Paulus for adultery and cited above (p. 20), that the statutory basis of the accusation brought before the *cognitio* needed to be specified; if it was not, the case could still be heard *extra ordinem*. In the case of Apuleius, the requirement to cite the relevant statute is potentially problematic, as magic was not covered in the text of any of the *publica iudicia* laws. It has been assumed (e.g. by Harrison 2001: 12) that the charge was brought under the Lex Cornelia on assassins and poisoners (and that it therefore would have been cited in the *libellus inscriptionis*).

Common to all early extensions of the Lex Cornelia is the charge that the alleged criminal activity led to, or was intended to lead to, the taking of life unlawfully. Paulus' *Sententiae*, from the end of the third century, made magic liable to criminal penalties (5.23) and the imperial Codes devoted named sections in their 'criminal book' (*CT* 9.16 = *CJ* 9.17) to magical practices and practitioners of magic. However, the direct evidence for the assimilation to the Lex Cornelia of the abuse of charms or poisons (*venena*), 'magical whisperings' or the sale of 'malign drugs' in public comes from the early sixth century (Just. *Inst.* 4.18.5). In Apuleius' time it was certainly possible to gloss the meaning of *venenum* and, in the process, establish a connection with magic and the occult (Rives 2003). Gaius' *Commentary on the Twelve Tables*, compiled probably at Rome, within a few years either way of Apuleius' trial, observed that the word *venenum* required qualification as 'good' or 'bad', as it could refer to beneficial drugs or poison (D. 50.16.236.pr.). Poisons and charms were also brewed up in secret, thus connecting them with the occult.

Senatorial, juristic and imperial rulings on the Lex Cornelia provide little support for the early inclusion of magic within its remit until the early third century, when Modestinus attests that 'evil sacrifices' were condemned to the *poena* of the Lex Cornelia (D. 48.8.13). The passage from Justinian which alone links magic explicitly with the Lex Cornelia cannot be cited for court practice four hundred years before. Moreover, if the relevant statute were the Lex Cornelia, we would expect argument as to the extent to which Apuleius' magical practices, even if proved to be unlawful, were designed to take human life. Yet Apuleius' defence is not directed against accusations of intended murder-by-magic, but the practice of magic arts *per se*, for unknown (but doubtless malevolent) ends. The strongest indication that the judge, at least, may have perceived the issue as being whether Apuleius had in fact killed someone through magic emerges in his intervention to interrogate a witness about whether an alleged victim had died as a result of Apuleius' spells: Maximus had asked the prosecution, in a rapid exchange (*Apol.* 48.7), why Apuleius had enchanted her (answer: to make her collapse), whether she had died (answer: no), and, in that case, what use it was to Apuleius anyway (no answer given). The orator cites this as an example of the governor's acuteness as a judge, not as an element central to the case.

At no point does he mention or address the Lex Cornelia, or any other criminal statute which might be concerned with magic. In three places he argues by analogy with other offences: first, murder, poisoning and theft (*Apol.* 26.2); second, piracy, theft and murder (32.2); and, third, violence (47.1). His selection does not suggest that he or his public were seriously concerned about juristic distinctions between the *publica iudicia* on murder and violence and the rest. He avoids mention of statute law, with one perhaps surprising exception (*Apol.* 47.4):

That magic of yours, as I hear, is a matter covered by the laws. From Antiquity onwards, it was forbidden by the Twelve Tables on account of the power of incantations directed against crops. Therefore, too, it is no less secret than frightful and horrible, as a rule practised in the watches of the night, hidden in shadow, isolated from witnesses, whispered in incantations.

This was not to suggest that the accusers had lodged a charge of magic, citing the Twelve Tables in the *inscriptio* as their statutory authority. Rather, it points to a more subtle working of the criminal-justice system, in which continuing social disapproval of magical and occult practices was given a quasi-legal sanction by reference to the Twelve Tables. Although no longer operative, the Twelve Tables had continued relevance to living law; their contents on theft and other matters puzzled the antiquarian and private-law judge Aulus Gellius, and the Code was the subject of commentaries by jurists at Rome in the first and second centuries AD. Therefore all concerned with Apuleius' case were agreed that the governor was empowered to judge on a charge of magic and that magic was illegal. The absence of a (recent) statute on magic was not in itself an obstacle to prosecution.

In his own defence Apuleius argued that the charges of magic were an invention, as the real grievance of his accusers was his marriage with Pudentilla and its financial consequences; the topics of marriage and money are handled in the second part of the speech. A charge of magic was 'more easily hinted at than proved' (*Apol.* 2) but the social stigma and fears attached to the occult made responses to it on the part of judges unpredictable (*Apol.* 42). He was the more vulnerable to such smears because he was an outsider. Arriving at Oea some three years before, he had been persuaded into the marriage by his friend Pontianus, Pudentilla's elder son, now deceased. His real accusers were Sicinius Aemilianus, the uncle of Apuleius' two stepsons and a greedy, obstreperous individual (*Apol.* 2), and Pontianus' father-in-law, Herennius Rufinus, both of whom wanted Pudentilla's money for themselves. He had become embroiled with them in a previous case a week earlier and they had thrown together the indictment (five charges and at least one witness statement), perhaps in the hope of exploiting the imminent arrival of the governor. For his part, Apuleius had no interest (he said) in his wife's money. Much of it had been settled on her sons when they married, and he would benefit from only a small legacy in her will. Extended explanation of his family's financial affairs was crucial to Apuleius' rebuttal of the charges; it established a motive for the accusation and subverted sympathy for the accusers by proving that their fears over the money were groundless.

The content of the prosecution speeches is known only from Apuleius' attempt to discredit them. Time limits, perhaps enforced through the use of a water clock, would have been imposed. On the pattern of the senatorial trials recorded by Pliny, the prosecution would have spoken first, followed by rebuttals from the defence, with testimony following at the end. At Apuleius' trial it is clear that the testimony was introduced as part of the presentations of the prosecution. Five allegations were made. First, Apuleius, the *magus* (magician), had bought fish for magical purposes (*Apol.* 29–41). Secondly, he had secretly bewitched a boy in a secret place (42–52). Third, he had wrapped up mysterious objects, along with Pontianus' household gods, in a linen cloth (53–4). Fourth, he had performed nocturnal sacrifices at the house of one Iunius Crassus; this had been evidenced by the presence of feathers and soot and was supported by a written statement from the owner of the house (57–60). Finally, Apuleius had manufactured a statue for magical purposes (61–5). In the course of their presentation, the proconsul had intervened to cross-question the accusers' advocate about the collapse of a second victim caused by Apuleius' magic (48).

As it stands, Apuleius' defence is, in general, to adopt the strategy of admitting that the allegations, with one exception, were true, but that they were not magic. The fish were for medical purposes – and anybody can go out and buy fish; the boy, Thallus, was an epileptic, so he was subject to falling fits; the objects wrapped up with the household gods were cultic souvenirs; and (the fifth charge) the wooden statuette was a charming little Mercury, produced in court. Only the charge of nocturnal sacrifices is denied outright. Although not given pride of place in Apuleius' account, it was far the most serious charge and also the best supported, as the prosecution had a witness statement. To provide a plausible reinterpretation of strange goings-on at night was not an option. Apuleius therefore insisted that the smoke and feathers were not admissible evidence and that the author of the witness statement was a drunken sot, who was probably still in bed and entirely unreliable.

Apuleius would not have been alone in his defence. Although invisible in the record, a professional advocate may have been employed to organise the technical aspects, such as the summoning and questioning of such witnesses as the doctor who testified to the epileptic conditions of Apuleius' alleged victims. Therefore, it was acceptable, in the context of the trial as a whole, that Apuleius has little to say about the law. Nor could a detailed exposition of the law be expected. As there was no statute on magic, there was no written set of definitions to set the terms of debate.

His approach therefore provides an example of how to address a 'social' crime, drawing on shared beliefs about what magic was, for example that the contact of magicians with the gods gave them power (*Apol.* 26.6). But the main concentration of Apuleius' defence is on his character, the reason why his version of his shopping for fish, and so on, should be believed over that of his opponents. The ornamentation of his speech with quotations from Plato, other philosophers and poets is designed to enhance his reputation as a man of culture, who shared the values of the Mediterranean elite, as also is his flattery of the governor and his *consilium*. Conversely, his main opponent, Aemilianus, is represented as greedy and uncivilised. Worse, he had been rude to the Prefect of the City at Rome when involved in a challenge to a will, a case (rightly) thrown out by the irate magistrate (*Apol.* 2). No judge could take seriously such a bore when compared with the eloquent and cultured defendant.

MAGIC AND DEVIANCE

Apuleius' defence was successful (as it is assumed), because he persuaded his audience that he was not the 'type' to engage in dangerous magic, despite his obvious knowledge of it. Rather, he was a virtuous member of society. The danger to Apuleius, however, which may have been greater than he admitted, was that he was an outsider, an unknown, of whom damaging allegations might be made with impunity. As so much of the outcome depended on perceptions of character, apparent departures from the norm could well have resulted in the victimisation of the innocent. Beyond the imperial entourage, the culture of which was inevitably shaped by the requirements of imperial security, the persecution of eccentricity – notably, but not exclusively, that of the Christians – was driven by perceptions of deviance.

Deviance is a social concept and has no place in any law. Yet the dividing line between the odd or eccentric or immoral but legal on the one side, and the unlawful on the other, could be a narrow one. Concepts of deviance are defined by the community, which labels certain activities and behaviours as deviant. On this theory, taken to extremes, there is no independent standard of morality by which actions may be defined as 'bad', only the standards imposed by a society at any given time (Becker 1963: 8–9):

Social groups create deviance by making the rules whose infraction constitutes deviance and by applying those rules to particular people and labelling them as outsiders. From this point of view, deviance is not a quality of the act the person commits but rather the consequence of the application by others of rules and sanctions to an 'offender'. The deviant is one to whom that label has successfully been applied; deviant behaviour is behaviour that people so label.

Deviance-theory has also tried to analyse the process of 'labelling', which occurs through a process of social negotiation. 'Moral entrepreneurs', in Becker's phrase, identify target groups as 'deviant' and embark on the process of creating or refining a social consensus which will result in the labelling of a group as 'deviant', or even unlawful (Prus and Grills 2003: 31–70).

The process of 'labelling', to be successful, must exploit existing prejudice but must also seek to persuade on its own account; in other words, some activity on the part of the 'moral entrepreneurs' is required for ideas of deviance to take hold. The theory assumes that the agents, who initiate the process and perpetuate it, are visible and not alone, working perhaps within organisational structures (such as those which make and administer the law), which assist them but cannot determine the outcome. The motives of the 'entrepreneurs' may be to enhance their own power and influence and oppress or exploit those weaker than themselves.

Four stages in the construction of a 'deviant' social identity have been identified (Prus and Grills 2003: 71–84): *typing*, whereby the agent reaches a private definition of a target; *designation*, when the agent makes his views known to others; *assessment*, as the view taken of the deviant 'target' is further considered and refined; and *resistance*, when the objects of the initial designation fight back. The last qualification is important for how labelling works in both individual cases and groups, and over time. For example, on the individual level, Apuleius resisted the implication of religious deviance present in the charge of magic brought against him by employing several strategies: while 'bad' magic was deviant, his actions did not fall into that category; and the reason why he should be believed was that one who can cite Plato and Ennius with eloquence and conviction was not the *type* to engage in deviant activity. Among groups, the Christians were liable to be labelled as 'deviant' because their beliefs and cultic practices were suspect; they appeared anti-social and secretive to their fellow-citizens and failed to observe public religious rites, including those honouring the emperor. Their perceived 'atheism' was also dangerous for social wellbeing, as it risked incurring the anger of the gods. But they did not accept their role as 'targets' passively, and second-century Christian apologetic literature devoted itself seriously to resisting the label of 'deviant' imposed on the religion, ultimately successfully.

Deviance theory may overplay the role of the persuading agent. No public orator was needed to create fear of magical and occult practices or the divine wrath. But public oratory and other forms of social conditioning on the part of the elite did frequently address the issue of deviance, seeking to label opponents as not only wrong but also types of whom society (in the shape of the judges and audience) would be expected to disapprove. Cicero's practice of attacking not only the case of his opponents but also their appearance, lifestyle, record in public life and character in general was designed not only to further his own cause, but also to deny them social support and approval. In extreme cases his attacks on political rivals, such as Catiline (in 63 BC), Antonius (in 44–43) and their supporters, were aimed at excluding them from the community itself. The function of punishment as example and deterrence (above, pp. 35–8) shows the importance attached to separating the 'virtuous' community from its delinquents.

The labelling of deviants was thus a contested process, which could take place in the context of social, religious or political competition. By exploiting social preconceptions and apprehensions, the labelling of opponents as deviants will help the 'agent' in a competitive process to win rewards in the shape of status, repute or recruits for oneself or one's own group at the expense of another. Once a person or group becomes socially suspect, their ability to function becomes impaired, and even innocent activities may become suspect or be used to discredit them (Prus and Grills 2003: 75). A more dangerous situation, for all parties, is created when competition becomes outright conflict, resulting in serious damage to one or both parties:

conflict is a one-on-one reciprocal antagonism, an exchange of injurious inten-tions and behaviours ... Competition occurs when the objective is not to hurt or diminish the opponent, but to capture a prize that both opponents wish to acquire ... Thus a sports contest or a love triangle represents competition, while a war or a brawl or a personal vendetta represents conflict. (Gilmore 1987: 13)

The importance of the concept of deviance is that there is no requirement for the deviant to have acted unlawfully for 'punishment' to occur. If the Christians, or other strange cults, were perceived as offering competition to the prevalent religious climate, as well as to specific beliefs (such as the imperial cult), they ran the risk of being labelled as deviant. If they were seen as being in conflict with prevailing attitudes because they denied the exis-tence of all gods but their own, the reaction was likely to be more extreme.

In the case of Apuleius, he was not only a stranger but, as a 'philosopher', also a member of a calling which could be socially suspect. 'No one', wrote

Ulpian, 'is punished for thinking' (D. 48.19.18) but some systems of thought, when indulged in by certain categories of people, encouraged suspect actions. Stoicism was an established and intellectually respectable philosophical school; Marcus Aurelius' Stoic beliefs as laid out in his *Meditations* reinforced his already high reputation. However, under Roman emperors in the first century, and especially Nero and Domitian, the stern moral code once championed by the younger Cato, self-styled martyr for the Republic, could be perceived as encouraging subversion (Macmullen 1966: 46–94; Brunt 1975). Therefore, when held by dissident senators, it was potentially a deviant belief, which could attract the unwelcome attention of the law – as administered by an emperor with complete discretion as to how it was enforced. Allegations of 'wrong' beliefs fuelled the charges brought against the senators Rubellius Plautus (Tac. *Ann.* 14.59) and Thrasea Paetus (*Ann.* 16.22) under Nero, as they did also the prosecution of Helvidius Priscus (Tac. *Hist.* 4.5). Romans did not punish 'thinking' but they did punish the actions which resulted from thinking. 'Wisdom', observed Demetrius the Cynic according to a later author, 'is now a crime' (Philostratus, *Life of Apollonius of Tyana* 7.11; Dio 65.13.1).

External appearance on its own could signal oddity, perhaps criminality. Vespasian, although secure in power and relatively tolerant of opposition, exiled philosophers in 71 because, according to Dio, who reflects the attitudes of the third century, his kingmaker Licinius Mucianus had described philosophers to the emperor as arrogant, rude and unkempt (Dio 65.13). Taken further, eccentricity might also be an indicator of more dangerous tendencies towards treason, for example, or magic. The Severan biographer of sophists, Philostratus, in an account of his hero, the philosopher and wonder-worker Apollonius of Tyana, conceded that Apollonius' matted hair and unkempt attire formed a plausible ancillary charge when he was hauled before Domitian on charges of illegal divination, human sacrifice and treason (*Life of Apollonius* 7.8–20). In Gaul in the 380s the local emperor, Maximus, threatened to hunt down and execute as heretics people with pale faces and ragged clothes (Sulpicius Severus, *Chronicle* 2.50.4; cf. Jerome, *Letters* 22.14). The threat was taken seriously, though not, in the event, put into practice, because Maximus had already found guilty of magic several individuals accused by their fellow-Christians of heresy (Chadwick 1978: 138–48); allegations of 'wrong belief' had merged with allegations of deviant practices to produce a capital charge, leading to the execution of the suspects.

Although both Philostratus' Apollonius and Apuleius before Claudius Maximus have more than an air of unreality, the emphasis on matters apparently extraneous to the main charges, which establish the good character of the defendant and his membership of the social (or philosophical) mainstream, illustrate the impact on the operation of justice of extra-legal factors. There is a sense also that some philosophers, who were wanderers and thus strangers in the communities they visited, were a type of people who could be at risk if the locals, for whatever reason, turned against them. The criteria used by society to construct the deviant are not those used by the law, but if governors were confronted with strong outbreaks of social outrage against perceived 'deviant' groups and individuals, the will of the people could become the law.

CONCLUSION

The connection between law and crime was an uneasy one. Roman authority was spread too thinly to police the summary justice exercised by local communities through their own courts or the lynch mob. Even where governors were present, they were sometimes prone to seek popularity, or yield to crowd pressure to avoid further disturbances. When apparent ignorance on the part of some governors of even basic legal principles is added, it should not surprise that law in action was on occasion unpredictable.

Crime, ultimately, was what the community judged to be wrong and the community could take the law into its own hands, perhaps by stoning a suspected wrongdoer (Pease 1907). In a society which claimed respect for the rule of law, the statutes and their interpreters provided a framework for public criminal justice, and Apuleius' parodies of the public trial show that the procedures were well understood by his readers. But all must have understood also how incomplete that framework was. Rules, if not broken, were constantly tested in the courts. Enterprising accusers would try their luck before the governor, to test how strict his interpretation of statute might prove. Strangers, eccentrics, women alone who brewed potions for the credulous, followers of secretive cults, and any others who exhibited deviant behaviour might find themselves the subject of social disapproval, leading to formal denunciation.

Discussion of the rules about what crime was at any period and how it was dealt with can therefore be only part of the picture of criminal and unlawful behaviour in the Roman world. The choice of which activities to 'criminalise' is itself a comment on the society which selects them, and the omissions too can be instructive: Rome did not worry, for example, about 'war crimes' or genocide, although it was concerned about the justification for war. In a violent and male-dominated society, rules on violence started from the premise that some forms of direct action were acceptable; the aim of regulation was to curtail its abuse. Notions of corruption were erratic because the requirement of the rules, that all be treated fairly, conflicted with the discretionary character of patronage; it may be no coincidence that complaints about corruption are heard most loudly from the most rule-bound period of Roman history, the Later Empire. Regulation of sexual behaviour was rooted in the Roman institution of the *familia* and attitudes of men towards women. In general the law was designed by the elite, largely for the elite, although its principles were universal, hence the connection, made by the elite writers, between virtue and social status and the assumption that the rights to dignity in punishment even of the most depraved *honestior* were superior to those of the lower classes.

When Justinian codified extracts from the jurists on delict and public offences, he described the result as his 'Books of Terror' (*Libri Terribiles*). The public exercise of criminal process was designed to impress upon the onlookers both the justice and the terror of the Roman system. But repeatedly criminal trials in the Roman Forum, the imperial Senate and the courts of the provincial governors showed the unpredictability of the outcome. From their very different perspectives, the authors of the Gospels on the trial of Jesus and Apuleius on fantasy justice show that the innocent too had good cause to be afraid.

Bibliographical essay

LEGAL TEXTS AND TRANSLATIONS

The Roman statutes, mainly from the Republic, are comprehensively edited and translated with extensive commentary by Michael Crawford and others (1996, abbreviated as *RS*). These and other early legal sources are also printed in Latin in S. Riccobono and others, eds., *Fontes Iuris Romani Anteiustiniani (FIRA)*, volume I (Florence, 1968–9). Justinian's *Corpus Iuris Civilis* contains the Digest (D.), the *Codex Justinianus (CJ)* and the *Institutes* (Just. *Inst.*): volume I, the Digest and *Institutes*, was edited by Th. Mommsen and P. Krueger; volume II, the *Codex Justinianus*, by P. Krueger; and volume III, ed. R. Schöll and W. Kroll, contains the *Novellae* ('new laws'). There is an *editio maior* of the Digest edited by Th. Mommsen (Berlin, 1870) and of the *Codex Justinianus* by P. Krueger (Berlin, 1877, repr. 1967). The text of the Theodosian Code (*CT*), which is not complete, was edited by Th. Mommsen, P. Meyer and P. Krueger (Berlin, 1905); Krueger also tried to further reconstruct the text by incorporating entries from the *CJ* which may have existed in the original *CT* (volume I, Books 1–6, Berlin, 1923). Otto Lenel reconstructed the surviving writings of the jurists by author, incorporating legal citations from other writers in his *Palingenesia Iuris Civilis* (1889); this provides an effective reminder that the jurists are in fact 'fragmentary authors' and removes them from the perhaps distorting effects of their context in the Digest. Gaius, *Institutes* exists in several editions; an accessible text is the Teubner version.

The Digest was translated into English by Alan Watson and others (Pennsylvania, 1985), Justinian's *Institutes* most recently by P. Birks and G. MacLeod (London, 1987, repr. 1994), and Gaius, *Institutes* by W. M. Gordon and Olivia Robinson (London, 1988). The Theodosian Code exists in a translation with brief notes by Clyde Pharr (Princeton, 1952, repr. New York 1969). There are also useful translations of selected texts.

On family law useful collections have been published by B. W. Frier and
T. A. J. McGinn, *A Casebook on Roman Family Law* (Oxford, 2004), which
provides guidance on how to think about legal texts in general, and by
J. Evans Grubbs, *Women and the Law in the Roman Empire* (2002).

MODERN WORKS: GENERAL

Olivia Robinson's *The Criminal Law of Ancient Rome* (1995) is the starting
point for a comprehensive survey of ancient writing on the criminal law,
and R. Bauman, *Crime and Punishment in Ancient Rome* (1996), has some
useful insights. Professor Robinson's more recent book, *Penal Practice and
Penal Policy in Ancient Rome* (2006), provides a set of case studies, including Ciceronian murder trials, the trial of Piso in AD 20, and trials for
extortion in the early second century AD and for treason and magic in the
fourth, through which changes in punishment practice evolved.

CHAPTERS 1–2

On Roman law in general, two good introductory books are O. Robinson,
The Sources of Roman Law: Problems and Issues for Ancient Historians (1997)
and D. Johnston, *Roman Law in Context* (1999), which focuses on the civil
law, with especial attention to commerce. For more detail W. W.
Buckland, *A Textbook of Roman Law*, ed. P. Stein (1966), is a mine of
information, although daunting for the non-specialist. For the culture of
the jurists F. Schultz, *History of Roman Legal Science* (Oxford, 1946), is still
reliable, although, for the historian, some of his judgements are controversial. I have recently published thoughts on Roman Republican legal
culture (*Cicero and the Jurists*, London, 2006). Tony Honoré's studies of
Gaius (Oxford, 1962) and of *Ulpian* (2nd edn, Oxford, 2004) are important, if controversial, studies of both jurists; Ulpian in particular is viewed
in the context of Roman perceptions of human rights. Alan Watson's
various monographs (see References) are invaluable for the law of the
Roman Republic, usually not covered as a separate topic in the literature;
see also Cloud (1994). On the role of advocacy in the Republic see Powell
and Paterson, eds., *Cicero the Advocate* (2004), and for the input of
advocates into legal discourse, along with significant discussion of the
contribution of Quintilian, J. Crook, *Legal Advocacy in the Roman World*
(1995); his *Law and Life of Rome* (London, 1967) seeks to set the workings of
Roman law in a wider social context.

CHAPTER 3

The connection of penal policy with social status is explored by Garnsey (1970); in general for punishment, see Bauman (1996); Harries (1998): 144–52; Robinson (2006). On torture, Page duBois, *Torture and Truth* (1991), explores the ethical ramifications of judicial and other forms of torture; for Late Antiquity, see also MacMullen (1986) and Clark (2006). The Romans distinguished judicial torture from the infliction of pain in the arena, for which see Coleman (1990, 1998) and Wistrand (1992).

CHAPTER 4

On delict and its subsequent history in the legal tradition, the classic work is R. Zimmermann, *The Law of Obligations* (1996); see also for the Republic, A. Watson, *The Law of Obligations in the Later Roman Republic* (1964). Gaius, *Institutes*, is as good a guidebook to Roman law as any modern work, covering delict and its history in Book 3. On Aulus Gellius (text and translation available in the Loeb Classical Library) see L. Holford-Strevens (2003) and, edited by the same author and A. Vardi, *The Worlds of Aulus Gellius* (Oxford, 2004).

CHAPTER 5

For bibliography and discussion of the *Repetundae* law see *Roman Statutes*, vol. I; also A. Lintott, *Judicial Reform and Land Reform in the Roman Republic* (Oxford, 1992). For Pliny's prosecutions and defences of various governors in the first decade of the second century AD, see the translation by B. Radice of *The Letters of the Younger Pliny*, in Penguin Classics (1963) and now Robinson (2006): ch. 4. On corruption in general see, briefly, C. Kelly in *Oxford Classical Dictionary* (3rd edn, Oxford, 1996): 402–3, s.v. corruption, and, for Late Antiquity, Ramsay MacMullen, *Corruption and the Decline of Rome* (1988), modified by Harries (1998).

CHAPTER 6

R. Bauman's study of the *crimen maiestatis* (1967) is thorough but may speculate more than the evidence allows. Levick (1976) is illuminating on treason under Tiberius and its antecedents, and Rutledge (2001) explains the mechanics and motivation of accusations. On the law of treason, see Robinson (1995): ch. 5; and (2006): ch. 3 (Piso in AD 20) and ch. 6, which explores the connection between magic and treason in Late Antiquity. Fuller accounts of the political background to the trial of Arvandus are found in Harries (1992).

CHAPTER 7

On women and law in general see Jane Gardner, *Women in Roman Law and Society* (London, 1986), which has material on adultery. On marriage and the family in the classical period, S. Treggiari, *Roman Marriage: Iusti Coniuges from the Time of Cicero to the Time of Ulpian* (1991), is the standard work; for Late Antiquity, see Arjava (1996) and Evans Grubbs (1995). For women often on the wrong side of the rules, T. A. J. McGinn on *Prostitution, Sexuality and the Law in Ancient Rome* (1998) is a brilliant study, supplemented by Rebecca Flemming's article on the sex trade in *JRS* 89 (1999): 38–61.

CHAPTER 8

Andrew Lintott's *Violence in Republican Rome* (2nd edn, 1999b) is the study of first resort for the Republic. For the Later Empire, various issues are raised in a collection of conference papers edited by H. Drake, *Violence in Late Antiquity: Perceptions and Practices* (2006), which deals with violence and its justification in some contexts; see also on Late Antiquity Gaddis (2005). On policing Rome see Nippel (1984) and for Caecina and the interdict on armed violence, Frier (1985).

CHAPTER 9

On homicide Cicero's defence speeches for alleged homicides are translated by Michael Grant in the Penguin Classics, *Cicero, Murder Trials*; there are also Penguin translations of Philostratus' *Life of Apollonius* and of Apuleius' *Metamorphoses*. Apuleius' *Apology* was edited by V. Huninck in 1997, and his English translation is to be found in S. Harrison and others, *Apuleius: Rhetorical Works* (2000). Riggsby (1999) is perceptive on the political and social context of the Lex Cornelia. Gordon (1999) provides an accessible and detailed consideration of the background on magic, and Bradley (1997) evokes the physical and cultural context of Apuleius' trial. On deviance theory there is a wide and growing literature, but basic works are those of Becker (1963) and Prus and Grills (2003).

References

Allison, J. E. and Cloud, J. D. (1962) 'The Lex Iulia Maiestatis', *Latomus* 21: 711–31

Arjava, A. (1996) *Women and Law in Late Antiquity*. Oxford

Aubert, J.-J. (2002) 'A Double Standard in Roman Criminal Law? The Death Penalty and Social Structure in Late Republican and Early Imperial Rome', in Aubert, J.-J. and Sirks, B., eds., *Speculum Iuris*. Michigan: 94–133

Badian, E. (1957/1964) 'Caepio and Norbanus', *Historia* 6: 318–46 = *Studies in Greek and Roman History* (1964): 34–70

Balsdon, J. P. V. D. (1938) 'The History of the Extortion Court at Rome 123–70 BC', *PBSR* 14: 98–114

Bauman, R. A. (1967) *The Crimen Maiestatis in the Roman Republic and Augustan Principate*. Johannesburg

 (1968) 'Some Remarks on the Structure and Survival of the *Quaestio de adulteriis*', *Antichthon* 2: 68–93

 (1980) 'The *Leges Iudiciorum Publicorum* and Their Interpretation in the Republic, Principate and Early Empire', *ANRW* II.13: 103–233

 (1996) *Crime and Punishment in Ancient Rome*. London

Beard, M. (1980) 'The Sexual Status of Vestal Virgins', *JRS* 70: 12–27

 (1994) 'Re-Reading (Vestal) Virginity', in Hawley, R. and Levick B., eds., *Women in Antiquity. New Assessments*. London: 166–77

Becker, H. S. (1963) *Outsiders. Studies in the Sociology of Deviance*. London

Bohannan, P. (1965) 'The Differing Realms of the Law', in Nader, L., ed., *The Ethnography of Law, American Anthropologist*, vol. 67.6.2: 33–42

Bradley, K. R. (1997) 'Law, Magic and Culture in the *Apologia* of Apuleius', *Phoenix* 51: 202–23

Briquel, D. (1980) 'Sur le mode d'exécution en cas de parricide et en cas de perduellio', *MÉFRA* 92: 87–107

Browning, R. (1952) 'The Riot of AD 387 in Antioch: the Role of the Theatrical Claque in the Later Empire', *JRS* 42: 13–20

Brunt, P. A. (1961) 'Charges of Provincial Maladministration under the Early Principate', *Historia* 10: 189–227

 (1975) 'Stoicism and the Principate', *PBSR* 43: 7–35

Buckland, W. W. (1966) *A Textbook of Roman Law*, ed. P. Stein. 3rd edn. Cambridge

Buti, I. (1982) 'La cognitio extra ordinem da Augusto a Diocleziano', *ANRW* II.14: 29–59

Chadwick, H. (1978) *Priscillian of Avila. The Occult and the Charismatic in the Early Church*. Oxford

Clark, G. (2006) 'Desires of the Hangman: Augustine on Legitimized Violence', in Drake ed. 2006: 137–46

Cloud, J. D. (1968) 'How Did Sulla Style His Law *de sicariis?*', *CR* n.s.18: 140–3

    (1969) 'The Primary Purpose of the Lex Cornelia *de sicariis*', *ZRG* 86: 258–86

    (1971) 'Parricidium: from the Lex Numae to the Lex Pompeia *de parricidiis*', *ZRG* 88: 1–16

    (1988) 'Lex Julia *de vi* – I', *Athenaeum* 66: 579–95

    (1989) 'Lex Julia *de vi* – II', *Athenaeum* 67: 427–65

    (1994) 'The Constitution and Public Criminal Law', in *CAH*, 2nd edn, vol. IX: 491–530

Coleman, K. (1990) 'Fatal Charades: Roman Executions Staged as Mythological Enactments', *JRS* 80: 44–73

    (1998) 'The Contagion of the Throng: Absorbing Violence in the Roman World', *Hermathena* 164: 65–88

Colin, J. (1965) 'Apulée en Thessalie: fiction ou vérité?', *Latomus* 24: 330–45

Cornell, T. (1981) 'Some Observations on the "Crimen Incesti"', in *Le délit religieux dans la cité antique*. Rome, 27–39

Crawford, M. H. and others (1996) eds. *Roman Statutes*. London

Crook, J. A. (1995) *Legal Advocacy in the Roman World*. London

Dickison, S. (1973) 'Abortion in Antiquity', *Arethusa* 6: 158–66

Dionisotti, A. C. (1982) 'From Ausonius' Schooldays? A Schoolbook and Its Relatives', *JRS* 72: 83–125

Drake, H. A. (2006) ed. *Violence in Late Antiquity. Perceptions and Practice*. Ashgate

duBois, Page (1991) *Torture and Truth*. London

Evans Grubbs, J. (1989) 'Abduction Marriage in Antiquity: a Law of Constantine and Its Social Context', *JRS* 79: 59–83

    (1995) *Law and Family in Late Antiquity. The Emperor Constantine's Marriage Legislation*. Oxford

    (2002) *Women and Law in the Roman Empire*. London

Ferrary, J.-L. (1983) 'Les origines de la loi de majesté à Rome', *CR Acad. Inscr.*: 556–72

    (1991) 'Lex Cornelia *de sicariis et de veneficis*', *Athenaeum* 79: 417–34

Flemming, R. (1999) '*Quae corpore quaestum facit*: the Sexual Economy of Female Prostitution in the Roman Empire', *JRS* 89: 38–62

Foucault, M., tr. Sheridan, A. (1977) *Discipline and Punish. The Birth of the Prison*. London

Fraschetti, A. (1984) 'La sepoltura delle Vestali e la città', in *Du châtiment dans la cité. École française de Rome*: 97–129

Frier, B. (1985) *The Rise of the Roman Jurists*. Princeton

Gaddis, M. (2005) *There Is No Crime for Those Who Have Christ: Violence in the Christian Roman Empire*. Berkeley

Garnsey, P. D. A. (1967) 'Adultery Trials and the Survival of the *Quaestiones* in the Severan Age', *JRS* 57: 56–60

(1968) 'Why Penal Laws Became Harsher: the Roman Case', *Natural Law Forum*: 141–62

(1970) *Social Status and Legal Privilege in the Roman Empire*. Oxford

(2004) 'Roman Citizenship and Roman Law', in Swain, S. and Edwards, C., eds., *Approaching Late Antiquity. The Transformation from Early to Late Empire*. Oxford: 133–55

Gilmore, D. (1987) *Aggression and Community*. New Haven, CT.

González, J. (1986) 'The Lex Irnitana: a New Copy of the Flavian Municipal Law', *JRS* 76: 147–243

Gordon, R. (1999) 'Imagining Greek and Roman Magic', in Ankarloo, B. and Clark, S., eds., *The Athlone History of Witchcraft and Magic in Europe*, vol. II: *Ancient Greece and Rome*. London: 159–276

Greenidge, A. H. J. (1901/1971) *The Legal Procedure of Cicero's Time*. London and Oxford

Griffin, M. (1973) 'The Tribune C. Cornelius', *JRS* 63: 196–213

Gruen, E. (1965) 'The Exile of Metellus Numidicus', *Latomus* 24: 576–80

(1968a) *Roman Politics and the Criminal Courts, 149–78*. Cambridge, MA

(1968b) 'M. Antonius and the Trial of the Vestal Virgins', *Rh. Mus.* III: 59–63

Harries, J. (1992) 'Sidonius Apollinaris, Rome and the Barbarians: a Climate of Treason?', in Drinkwater, J. and Elton, H., eds., *Fifth-Century Gaul: a Crisis of Identity?* Cambridge: 298–308

(1994) *Sidonius Apollinaris and the Fall of Rome*. Oxford

(1998) *Law and Empire in Late Antiquity*. Cambridge

(1999) 'Constructing the Judge: Judicial Accountability and the Culture of Criticism in Late Antiquity', in Miles, R., ed., *Constructing Identities in Late Antiquity*. London: 214–33

(2006a) *Cicero and the Jurists*. London

(2006b) 'Violence, Victims and the Legal Tradition in Late Antiquity', in Drake ed. 2006: 83–100

Harrison, S. and others (2001) *Apuleius: Rhetorical Works*. Oxford

Hobsbawn, E. J. (1969) *Bandits*. London

Holford-Strevens, L. (2003) *Aulus Gellius. An Antonine Scholar and His Achievement*. 2nd edn. Oxford

Honoré, T. (1998) *Law in the Crisis of Empire 379–455 AD. The Theodosian Dynasty and Its Quaestors*. Oxford

Hopwood, K. (1989) 'Bandits, Elites and Rural Order', in Wallace-Hadrill, A., ed., *Patronage in Ancient Society*. London: 171–88

(1998) 'All That May Become a Man: the Bandit in the Ancient Novel', in Foxhall, L. and Salmon, J., eds., *When Men Were Men. Power and Identity in Classical Antiquity*. London: 195–204

Isaac, B. (1984) 'Bandits in Judaea and Arabia', *Harv. Stud.* 88: 171–203

Johnston, D. (1999) *Roman Law in Context*. Cambridge

Jones, A. H. M. (1964) *The Later Roman Empire. A Social, Economic and Administrative History*. Oxford

(1972) *The Criminal Courts of the Roman Republic and Principate*. Oxford

Kallett-Marx, R. (1990) 'The Trial of P. Rutilius Rufus', *Phoenix* 44: 122–39

Katzoff, R. (1972) 'Precedents in the Courts of Roman Egypt', *ZRG* 89: 256–92
  (1980) 'Sources of Law in Roman Egypt: the Role of the Prefect', *ANRW* II.13: 807–44

Lempert, R. and Sanders, J. (1989) *An Invitation to Law and Social Science*. Philadelphia

Lenel, O. (1889) *Palingenesia Iuris Civilis*. Leipzig

Levick, B. (1976) *Tiberius the Politician*. London
  (1979) '*Poena legis maiestatis*', *Historia* 28: 358–79

Lewis, R. G. (2006) ed. *Asconius. Commentaries on Speeches by Cicero*. Oxford

Lintott, A. (1990) 'Electoral Bribery in the Roman Republic', *JRS* 80, 1–16
  (1994) 'Political History 146–95 BC', in *CAH*, 2nd edn., vol. IX: 40–104
  (1999a) *The Constitution of the Roman Republic*. Oxford
  (1999b[1968]) *Violence in Republican Rome*. 2nd edn. Oxford
  (2004) 'Legal Procedure in Cicero's time', in Powell and Paterson eds. 2004: 61–78

McGinn, T. (1998) *Prostitution, Sexuality and the Law in Ancient Rome*, Oxford

MacMullen, R. (1966) *Enemies of the Roman Order: Treason, Unrest and Alienation in the Empire*. Cambridge, MA
  (1986) 'Judicial Savagery in the Roman Empire', *Chiron* 16: 147–66
  (1988) *Corruption and the Decline of Rome*. Yale

Matthews, J. (1989) *The Roman Empire of Ammianus*. London

May, J. M. (1988) *Trials of Character: the Eloquence of Ciceronian Ethos*. Chapel Hill, NC

Millar, F. (1977) *The Emperor in the Roman World*. London
  (1981) 'The World of the Golden Ass', *JRS* 71: 63–75 = (2002) *Government, Society and Culture in the Roman Empire*: 313–35
  (1984) 'Condemnation to Hard Labour in the Roman Empire from the Julio-Claudians to Constantine', *PBSR* 52: 124–47 = (2002) *Government, Society and Culture in the Roman Empire*: 120–50
  (1998) *The Crowd in Rome in the Late Republic*. Ann Arbor, MI

Momigliano, A. (1986) 'Religious opposition', *Opposition et résistances à l'empire d'Auguste à Trajan*. Fondation Hardt, Entretiens 33: 103–33

Morris, A. (1987) *Women, Crime and Criminal Justice*. London and New York

Mouritsen, H. (2001) *Plebs and Politics in the Late Roman Republic*. Cambridge

Nippel, W. (1984) 'Policing Rome', *JRS* 74: 20–9
  (1995) *Public Order in Ancient Rome*. Cambridge

Nörr, D. (1986) *Causa Mortis. Münchener Beiträge zur Papyrusforschung und antiken Rechtsgeschichte* 80. Munich

Orestano, R. (1980) 'La *cognitio extra ordinem*: una chimera', *Stud. Doc. Hist. Iur.* 46: 236–47

Peachin, M. (1996) *Iudex vice Caesaris. Deputy Emperors and the Administration of Justice during the Principate*. Stuttgart.

Pease, A. S. (1907) 'Notes on Stoning among the Greeks and Romans', *TAPA* 38: 5–18

Powell, J. and Paterson, J. (2004) eds. *Cicero the Advocate*. Oxford

Prus, R. and Grills, S. (2003) *The Deviant Mystique: Involvements, Realities and Regulation*. Westport, CT and London

Ramsay, John T. (2005) 'Mark Antony's Judicial Reform and Its Revival under the Triumvirs', *JRS* 95: 20–37

Rawson, E. (1974) 'Religion and Politics in the Late Second Century BC at Rome', *Phoenix* 28: 193–212

Richardson, J. S. (1983) 'The *Tabula Contrebiensis*: Roman Law in Spain in the Early First Century BC', *JRS* 73, 33–41

(1987) 'The Purpose of the Lex Calpurnia *de repetundis*', *JRS* 77: 1–12

(1997) 'The Senate, the Courts and the *SC de Pisone patre*', *CQ* 47.2: 510–18

Richlin, A. (1981) 'Approaches to the Sources on Adultery at Rome', in Foley, H., ed., *Reflections of Women in Antiquity*. Princeton: 379–404

(1992) 'Reading Ovid's Rapes', in Richlin, A., ed., *Pornography and Representation in Greece and Rome*. Oxford: 158–79

Riess, W. (2001) *Apuleius und die Räuber. Ein Beitrag zur historischen Kriminalitäsforschung*. Heidelberger Althistorische Beiträge und Epigraphische Studien 35. Stuttgart

Riggsby, A. (1999) *Crime and Community in Ciceronian Rome*. Texas

(2004) 'The Rhetoric of Character in the Roman courts', in Powell and Paterson eds. 2004: 165–86

Rives, J. B. (2003) 'Magic in Roman Law: the Reconstruction of a Crime', *Cl. Ant.* 22: 313–39

Rivière, Y. (2002) *Les délateurs sous l'empire romain*. Paris

Robinson, O. F. (1968) 'Private Prisons', *RIDA* 15: 389–98

(1995) *The Criminal Law of Ancient Rome*. London

(1997) *The Sources of Roman Law: Problems and Issues for Ancient Historians*. London

(2002) 'Quintilian and Adultery', in *Iurisprudentia Universalis. Festschrift Th. Mayer-Maly*. Cologne: 631–8

(2005) 'Quintilian's Use of Roman Law', in Tellegen-Couperus ed. 2005: 59–66

(2006) *Penal Practice and Penal Policy in Ancient Rome*. London

Rogers, R. S. (1933) *Criminal Trials and Criminal Legislation under Tiberius*. Ann Arbor, MI

Rutledge, S. H. (2001) *Imperial Inquisitions. Prosecutors and Informants from Tiberius to Domitian*. London

Santalucia, B. (1998) *Diritto e processo penale nell' antica Roma*. 2nd edn. Milan

Scafuro, A. (1997) *The Forensic Stage*. Cambridge

Shaw, B.(1984) 'Bandits in the Roman Empire', *Past and Present* 105: 3–52

(1993) 'Tyrants, Bandits and Kings: Personal Power in Josephus', *Journal of Jewish Studies* 44: 176–204

Sherwin White, A. N. (1956) 'Violence in Roman Politics', *JRS* 46: 1–9

(1963) *Roman Society and Roman Law in the New Testament*. Oxford

(1982) 'The Political Ideas of C. Gracchus', *JRS* 72: 18–31

Stewart, P. (1999) 'The Destruction of Statues in Late Antiquity', in Miles, R., ed., *Constructing Identities in Late Antiquity*. London: 159–89

References

Summers, R. G. (1970) 'Roman Justice and Apuleius' *Metamorphoses*', *TAPA* 101: 511–31

Tatum, W. J. (1996) *Clodius. The Patrician Tribune*. Chapel Hill, NC

Tellegen-Couperus, O. (1993) *A Short History of Roman Law*. London
(2005) ed. *Quintilian and the Law. The Art of Persuasion in Law and Politics.* Leuven

Thomas, J. A. C. (1975) *The Institutes of Justinian. Text, Translation and Commentary.* Amsterdam

Thomas, Y. (1981) 'Parricidium I. Le père, la famille et la cité (la Lex Pompeia et le système des poursuites publiques)', *MÉFRA* 93: 643–715

Treggiari, S. (1991) *Roman Marriage: Iusti Coniuges from the Time of Cicero to the Time of Ulpian.* Oxford

Turpin, W. (1991) 'Imperial Subscriptions and the Administration of Justice', *JRS* 81: 101–18

Van Dam, R. (1985) *Leadership and Community in Late Antique Gaul.* California

Vera, D. (1981) *Commento storico alle* Relationes *de Quinto Aurelio Simmaco.* Pisa

Watson, A. (1964) *The Law of Obligations in the Later Roman Republic.* Oxford
(1970) *The Law of the Ancient Romans.* Dallas
(1974) *Law Making in the Later Roman Republic.* Oxford

Wiseman, T. P. (1970) 'The Definition of *Eques Romanus*', *Historia* 19: 67–83

Wistrand, M. (1992) *Entertainment and Violence in Ancient Rome: the Attitudes of Roman Writers of the First Century* AD. Göteborg

Zimmermann, M. (2006) 'Violence Reconsidered', in Drake ed. 2006: 343–57

Zimmermann, R. (1996) *The Law of Obligations.* Oxford

Index